BUT...I ANOINTED

YOU!

BY
TAMARA J. HAWTHORNE

Jordi

You are the real Deal!
God Sees you and is with
you Every step of your
Journey.
Remember your mission is
from God NOT PEOPLE.
May God, in Jesus Name bless
you in Every Area.

Love Always!
Tommy —

TABLE OF CONTENTS

DEDICATION

his book is dedicated to the Lord Jesus Christ who has given me the privilege of having a front row seat in witnessing his awesomeness and supernatural power at work in my life and others'.

I also dedicate this book to my dearly beloved brother, Ethan Moore: your life and death impacted my life greatly. You I loved.

INTRODUCTION

1 Corinthians 1:26-29 says, "Remember, dear brothers and sisters, that few of you were wise in the world's eyes, or powerful, or wealthy when God called you. Instead, God deliberately chose things the world considers foolish in order to shame those who think they are wise. And he chose those who are powerless to shame those who are powerful. God chose things despised by the world, things counted as nothing at all, and used them to bring to nothing what the world considers important, so that no one can ever boast in the presence of God."

God uses the common, the ordinary, the forgotten, the rejected, the abused, the lost, the lonely, the unloved, and totally trampled upon people of this world—to accomplish the most wonderful, supernaturally awesome generational shifting miracles of God. God uses the common folks, like me and maybe you. God uses us because we are the most ordinary clay pots that by ourselves would never reflect God's brilliance. He does this so the strong and the wise bold ones of this world could never ever mistake our success and glory to be something that we manifested on our own. Simply put, the more common the vessel, the greater glory and honor God receives and deserves.

When God has anointed you for a purpose, a mission, the thing he created you to do, your life becomes a testimony to the magnificent power, grace, and love of God. You shine, and you move in the ability of Jesus Christ. I write this book because the Lord anointed me to do so; I am not a writer and was diagnosed years ago with Dyslexia. I failed English so many times, and if it were not for the gift of God called "spell check," this book might have taken another twenty years to complete.

However, none of that matters when God calls you to serve and move out in faith and his ability. It does not matter what family you were born into, what college you attended (If you attended college) God makes a way; he aligns you with every resource you will need from education to finances to get your mission accomplished. Why? Because it's not your mission, it is God's; you are only the means or the vehicle from which God operates. I have seen many things in my lifetime, much pain and sadness as well as good things, wonderful things, and there is nothing more satisfying and soul-fulfilling than being used by God for his purpose.

If you are courageous and step out in faith, all the emptiness that we as humans search everywhere to fill is filled to the brim by God. This is a continuous process that never gets old. God cannot use you without absorbing some of his light, his glory, and his awesomeness. It's like you glow from the light of God long after you have been used for his purposes.

So no excuse. Trust me; I thought of some whoppers when it comes to why I can't do the things God has called me to do. However, no excuses will change the fact that God *anointed you*!

CHAPTER 1:

GROUND WORK

I hope to inspire those who are tired of consuming spiritual milk and cry out for the solid food that only God offers to those who are willing to step out on faith. The more we fill ourselves with God's food, the greater our understanding becomes about Jesus and his plan for our lives. What was hazy will now come into clear focus. It is like when you're at your eye doctor's office and the eye doctor is testing what eye prescription lenses best suits you. The doctor test several different lenses and ask you to read the chart located on the wall in front of you. The letters you strain to see are out of focus and blurry until the eye doctor hits the correct lens prescription. The eye doctor does this several times, asking you each time, "Is it better this way or the other way?" Suddenly, when the eye doctor hits the correct lens-- boom, everything comes into focus immediately. What you could not see before is now clear. Once you have accepted Christ as your Savior and complete some ground work—then all God intended for your life comes into clear focus.

"Anyone who is willing to hear should listen and understand!" Matt. 13:9 But blessed are your, eyes, because they see; and your ears, because they hear. I assure you, many prophets and godly people have longed to see and hear what you have seen and heard, but they could not." -Matthew 13:16-17 (NLT)

The above scriptures are awesome. However, as I studied, it became clear that to understand and move forward in the mission God had in mind when he created you, **you** must first have an **intimate relationship with Jesus.** Jesus is the one thing we must *have* to have abundance and understanding. Jesus said, **"Whoever *has* will be given more, and they will have abundance." Whoever does not *have*, what they do *have* will be taken from them.** (Matthew 13:12) Once you establish a strong bond with Jesus, this relationship with him will position you to move forward into the mission that God has specially designed for you.

Your mission is the very reason why Jesus went to the cross and paid for your sins with his life. Every saved person should strive to complete their mission from God because it gives God the glory he totally deserves.

I think sometimes we forget how awesome the gift of salvation is: God gave us *eternity. Which means our souls will never die.* Our body will go to dust, but not the part that makes us who we are; *your soul.* As a police detective, I have unfortunately seen death come to the human body in all sorts of ways. From this, I have come to understand the soul and the body are two different entities. The untimely death of my dad was the first time I realized how distinctly different the human soul is from the body.

On Nov 13, 1992, after being told my dad was having trouble, I arrived at his home to find his body lying on the floor in his bedroom. As I entered the room, I felt what I know now to be a death spirit. It was not scary (at least not in this case), but it felt vacant and void. Absent, was the feelings of isolation or sadness, which I have felt on many suicide scenes. I felt as if I was in somebody else's house and bedroom rather than my dad's, even though I had been in Dad's bedroom many times in the past.

My dad was the type of man who brought life and fun to everything we did. One of my fondest memories of my dad as a child was going to the grocery store and running other mundane errands. He made it fun; I don't know how he did, but he did, right down to buying lunchmeat and bread from the grocery store and then sitting in the parking lot in his Cadillac, eating chipped ham sandwiches. I never knew this was done to save money. Since my dad's death, I have not been able to find a ham sandwich that tasted as good as they did when I ate them with my dad.

Much like my dad, his house was warm and alive, and it was an adventure to visit. I mainly lived with my mom. The house itself was a huge, drafty almost mansion type of house. At one time, long before I was born, my dad would take on boarders and operate a bed and breakfast. My dad's house also was directly next door to a funeral home/crematory, which was weird, but this did not diminish the warmth and love that emanated from his home. My dad had a sense of humor, and I as the good daughter, would laugh at the same joke he'd tell every time we passed the Cemetery. He would say, "You know, people are dying to get in there." This silly joke still makes me smile. It's amazing what you remember when a loved one dies. So I know if my dad could see himself lying on the floor dead, he would say, "Well, I don't have far to travel." He didn't; they came right over from the funeral home next door and prepared his body for his grand funeral that would follow.

My dad was a police officer also. He loved being a cop; he taught me so many lessons from why never to take a bribe to how to swing a nightstick. Apparently my dad had touched thousands of other people's lives too. His funeral had a police escort and thousands of people came to his funeral and services. If you saw the procession to the Cemetery, you would think the Mayor of a huge city or somebody equally as important had died. They would be correct; the man in the casket was somebody important—he was my dad.

My dad and I were always affectionate with each other. My dad was not by any means perfect, but he loved me and I loved him. This is a blessing that some never experience. My dad and I hugged often and told each other we loved each other. My father's death was unexpected, even though he did have a few heath issues. However, prior to his death; God gave me the honor and privilege of being the person who introduced my dad to Jesus Christ. It was the first time I ever saw him cry.

On this cold November day, I found myself standing in the doorway of my dad's bedroom, as I had done so many times in the past. The difference today was I stood in the bedroom doorway, looking at my dad's dead body on the floor. In a moment, my life had changed. I felt overwhelmed with a feeling of stillness, finality. This feeling almost sucked the air out of the room. It was me and him, the dad who, earlier that day, had called me to ask me to bring him some medicine because he didn't feel well. As I gained the courage and the ability to move my feet in a walking forward motion, I walked into the room toward my dad's body.

I decided to reach down and touch his hair; I loved his hair, which, at the age of seventy-three, was still gorgeous. He was a mixture of Irish, American Indian, and African American, so his hair was full, wavy, and beautiful. His hair was truly his crowning glory along with his greying mustache, making my dad a handsome man. Even as he lay motionless on the floor at seventy-three years old, he was still a handsome man. I instinctually reached down for my dad's hair, ever since I was a child, my dad not only allowed us to play with his hair, he encouraged it. He liked his scalp massaged and scratched a lot. He allowed his children to play with his hair, and he didn't mind if I put his hair into ponytails and other experimental hairstyles, as long as he got a scalp message out of the deal. My dad's hair and scalp I knew. He used to say jokingly, "I'll give you two hours to stop this now." It was just me and Dad in the bedroom as the bright sunlight shined through the windows onto my dad's dead body. My dad was in a holding pattern until the funeral director came from next door to pick up dad's body. I guess I wanted to touch his hair one last time before all the other craziness with his funeral preparations began.

As I reached my hands down and touched his hair, in that moment, I felt something strange. I can only explain this feeling to you by asking you to imagine riding on a public transportation bus, and for some odd reason, you decide to reach out and fondle the stranger's hair that happens to be sitting in front of you. Right, now you got the picture—this is what I felt immediately. I did not know this person; remember, I had not touched his skin, only his hair. I felt what seemed to me to be electrical, almost what it feels like if you put your tongue on a nine-volt battery. I felt only a slight jolt, but this still totally alarmed and overwhelmed me instantly. I heard in my soul (not an audible voice), but still clear, as if a person stood beside me in the room and whispered, "Your dad does not live here anymore; he's gone." I instantly understood "he's gone" to mean the piece of my father that made him my dad (his soul) was gone.

I quickly snatched my hand away and stumbled back a little to sit down on his bed, which was next to my dad's body. I sat there with his body until the funeral people came. My Uncle Howard also later joined me in my dad's bedroom. We both sat on dad's bed in silence. This experience with my dad totally rattled me. I never again tried to touch any part of my dad's body or anyone else's dead body again. I have come to understand the human body is simply a shell that houses our spirit, our soul. Once we die, our bodies must return to where they came from (dirt), but if you're a born-again believer in Jesus Christ, you shall dwell forever with our Lord.

"For we know that when this earthly tent we live in is taken down-when we die and leave these bodies-we will have a home in heaven, an eternal body made for us by God himself and not by human hands. We grow weary in our present bodies, and we long for the day when we will put on our heavenly bodies like new clothing. For we will not be spirits without bodies, but we will put on new heavenly bodies. Our dying bodies make us groan and sigh, but it's not that we want to die and have no bodies at all. We want to slip into our new bodies so that these dying bodies will be swallowed up by everlasting life. God himself has prepared us for this, and as a guarantee he has given us his Holy Spirit.

So we are always confident, even though we know that as long as we live in these bodies we are not at home with the Lord. That is why we live by believing and not by seeing. Yes, we are fully confident, and we would rather be away from these bodies, for then we will be at home with the Lord. So our aim is to please him always, whether we are here in this body or away from this body."
-2 Corinthians 5:1-9

Our souls have eternity simply because Jesus died for you and me. Jesus exchanged our sins for his grace. I often say God got the short end of the stick with me; I got the better deal. Think about it: our sin debt is *paid in full*, we are reconciled with our Holy Father, and our dirty filthy robes are exchanged for a white one. Grace and mercy are ours, along with **every promise** the word of God proclaims, belongs to us from the Old Testament to Revelation. No matter what type of day you are having, God is still worthy to be praised. Without Jesus, you are simply judged on your own merits of what good and what bad you have done in your life. This is a no brainer, and a win-win situation. God says every idle word he will judge. If words were my only issue, maybe I'd roll the dice, but with me and anyone who is humble enough to see yourself the way God sees your sin would choose God hands down.

"For if you confess with your mouth that Jesus is Lord and believe in your heart that God raised him from the dead, you will be saved. For it is by believing in your heart that you are made right with God, and it is by confessing with your mouth that you are saved." -Romans 10:9-10

"I assure you, anyone who believes in me already has eternal life." -John 6:47

CHAPTER 2:

SOMETHING FOR NOTHING

*U*nderstand once you have stepped into God's family by repenting your sins and truly accepting Jesus as your Savior, you have come into *agreement* with the Word of God. It is done; this gift is never taken back from you. **Salvation is free**; the **best gift *ever* is free**, given in love from Jesus Christ to you. However, growth in Christ will cost you. Your price to grow in God will be dying to self, which *will be* painful at times. The truth is, we as Christians can live as carnal Christians barely distinguishable from an unsaved person. That Christian who doesn't move forward in Christ is somewhat ineffective as a prayer warrior and/ or deliverance ministry. They are usually shifted to and fro with the wind of this world because their foundation is not stable. Nevertheless, if they died today, they are promised (by God) to be with the Lord. My question is why would you want to live life halfway? God designed us to live life abundantly and reap all the benefits Christ has to offer you.

"And I am convinced that nothing can ever separate us from his love. Death can't, and life can't. The angels can't, and the demons can't. Our fears for today, our worries about tomorrow, and even the powers of hell can't keep God's love away. Whether we are high above the sky or in the deepest ocean, nothing in all creation will ever be able to separate us from the love of God that is revealed in Christ Jesus our Lord." -Romans 8:38-39

The cost, the growth, is part two in living abundantly in Christ. Obtaining this is possible only through receiving the Holy Spirit. We will talk more about this, but remember God says, **"Not by might, not by power, but by my Holy Spirit it will be done."(Zechariah 4:6)** As a Christian, you have part one, but then you may wonder why, you're still in the same place year after year. Are you the person who rushes to the altar every time the pastor calls for people who need prayer to come up? Are you the person who keeps getting delivered and healed from the same issue? If so, you might be stuck. This is the season to get unstuck and get on with your mission. I talk to people every day who profess they are followers of Jesus Christ and go to church every Sunday, but don't have any idea what their mission is in God. If this is you, then now is the appointed time to take an inventory of your life. It's time to go to step two. If you have already been in this growth phase, but now feel idle or fallen back, it's okay. Our God is the God of second chances. For me, he's been a God of third, fourth, and fifth chances.

First Thing:

Who has the first position in your life? Create a list, with numbers one through five, with one being the person or thing most important to you. Please be honest; you will never move forward until you know exactly where you are now. Where you are at right now matters. Think about it—whenever you go to set a destination to any place you want to go, your GPS device or app will ask for your current location. You cannot set a destination to go anywhere unless you find out where you are *now*.

Many years ago, I counseled a woman who was having trouble in this area. I prayed with her and spoke with her often during the many crises in her life. One Sunday, she happened to sit by me at church. I noticed she arrived late for worship (which we all run late at times), but I got a feeling this was her normal routine. As the praise songs went into worship songs (praise songs come first because they celebrate how truly magnificent God is), the woman sat down and began to check her cell phone messages. She was beside me, so I could not help but notice. I was temporarily distracted as she openly laughed while she proceeded to respond back to her text messages. This is the same woman who spoke to me about how desperate she was to experience a mighty move of God in her life.

It dawned on me this was the problem: people want a mighty move of God, but they are not willing to pay the cost by putting God first. It should be noted when this woman's next crises escalated and we talked further, I (in love) asked her about her prayer and Bible reading habits. They did not exist. I offered to walk alongside her to teach her by example, the habit of learning how to worship, pray and read God's Word. Note: most times, Pressing into God doesn't come naturally to us as humans, so spirit filled mentors are necessary and so important. We have to learn how to pray and how to listen to the still voice of God.

I was blessed enough to have mentors who walked beside me and taught me. Sometimes it's not a matter of laziness; it is a matter of ignorance. It is a commitment; it is work to step from drinking milk as a baby Christian to eating meat as a mature Christian. By the way, this woman never called me again to pray for her, and she stopped attending church regularly. As I said, part two will cost you, but some are never willing to pay the price. Prayers from others are awesome, but it is our responsibility to pray for our own family and ourselves. We must do the groundwork.

"Then Jesus said to the disciples, "If any of you wants to be my follower, you must put aside your selfish ambition, shoulder your cross, and follow me." -Matthew 16:24

CHAPTER 3:

THE RESTLESS CHRISTIAN

*W*e discussed what a baby Christian is and what they drink. Like babies, they are quite comfortable with drinking milk. I feel this book is for meat eaters, those Christians who are willing to go into the deeper matters of God. I also see this person as a "Restless Christian." The Restless Christian cannot stay where they are because they crave the meatier things of God. The Holy Spirit will continually harass them to reach for the deeper things God has to offer. We meat eaters come in every color, shape, and age; we are the people who actively go after Jesus. This book is for the Christians that have caught a glimpse of what God has for them. This glimpse may come in the form of a dream, vision, or prophetic words. However, now that you got this glimpse, you are restless, not satisfied to remain where you are or have been year after year.

Sometimes God gives you a taste of what your mission is and what's coming; God gives you an expectant spirit. Just as a woman who is pregnant anticipates the birth of her child, so do those who are moved by faith to walk in the abundance of God. A person, who is anticipating a great move of God in their life, will barely be able to comprehend just the peak of this glimpse. This glimpse of what God has planned for you will be awesome and scary at the same time. The glimpse of your purpose will seem (as it was to me) ridiculously impossible. You know something big is coming, and you know it's something good, you know God is preparing you for your mission, the thing he created you to do. Yet, you have absolutely no idea how all this will occur. Whatever you're God designed mission is for your life, I promise it will totally fulfill you. Along with the restlessness, your craving to be obedient to God becomes greater; your craving for God's *will* becomes stronger, and you strive and grow toward the issues important to God. You will become about your Father's business.

This book is also for the person who knows what their mission is and is willing to do the work necessary to stay in the correct position. The correct position is directly under the flow or move of God when he begins the outpouring of his blessings. This person can be a male or female of any age. You might be the person who is formally educated or not, poor or rich. It doesn't matter who you are; what does matters is God knows you and knows what he created you to do. Whether you believe it or not, God did plan a destination for your life. This might be a comforting thought and know I do want my words to comfort you, but the truth of the matter is our mission from God is usually anything but comforting. God has anointed you, but the sad thing is that many of us Christians will die without ever realizing our destiny.

My brother Ethan was one of these people. He was saved, but never ever dwelled in the abundant existence God had for him. Your mission path is a narrow path to walk and dwell in; it will cost you, but the payout is beyond human understanding. Dying to self, simply put, at times it is uncomfortable and downright hurts. What I have found is dying to self must be done daily. However, it is your choice; it's all about choice with God. You can always choose the alternative path; this path is wide open and filled with great pleasure. It's easy, and it's comfortable and safe. If the hard path is not for you, then give this book to a Restless Christian you know, and I will see you later in heaven. God bless. However, if you choose the hard and narrow road, then get ready—it will soon be show time.

Your mission or the destination that God has created you to do will (in your human mind) look totally impossible, but God operates well in the impossible. That is why Jesus said with man, things are impossible, but with God, nothing is impossible. This is why God did what he did in Gideon's situation with his three hundred soldiers. No, not the three hundred Spartan soldiers from the battle of Thermopylae, which took, place about 480 BC; they made a pretty good Hollywood movie for this battle. No, I am talking about the battle that occurred centuries before this battle. Both battles displayed a great deal of courage on the soldier's part. The only difference is the outcome. Gideon's three hundred men *won*. They won for one simple reason: God was with them and he did the impossible.

With God, nothing **is impossible**; he's God. So many times in my life I have placed my own human limitations on God's *unlimited* ability. Big mistake. God is the one who created us, gravity, the universe; he created the laws by which the universe operates. So if you have that vision (which means you're old like me), the word of God says young men have dreams and old men have visions. Seriously, whether it's a dream, a vision, or a brief snap shot of your mission God created you to do it, so don't run. I know it's almost too awesome to think too long on, but maybe, God is saying to you what he said to me, "**BUT I ANOINTED YOU.**"

"So Jerubbaal (that is, Gideon) and his army got up early and went as far as the spring of Harod. The armies of Midian were camped north of them in the valley near the hill of Moreh. The Lord said to Gideon, "You have too many warriors with you. If I let all of you fight the Midianites, the Israelites will boast to me that they saved themselves by their own strength. Therefore, tell the people, 'Whoever is timid or afraid may leave and go home.'" Twenty-two thousand of them went home, leaving only ten thousand who were willing to fight. But the Lord told Gideon, "There are still too many! Bring them down to the spring, and I will sort out who will go with you and who will not." When Gideon took his warriors down to the water, the Lord told him, "Divide the men into two groups. In one group put all those who cup water in their hands and lap it up with their tongues like dogs. In the other group put all those who kneel down and drink with their mouths in the stream." Only three hundred of the men drank from their hands. All others got down on their knees and drank with their mouths in the stream. The Lord told Gideon, "With these three hundred men I will rescue you and give you victory over the Midianites. Send all the others home." So Gideon collected the provisions and rams' horns of the other warriors and sent them home. But he kept the three hundred men with him."-Judges 7:1-8

CHAPTER 4:

POWERED UP

*O*nce you come around to the idea that God did not create and save you to take up space in a church pew somewhere, God has created you for something totally fulfilling and special. You might be the person saying, "Yes, let's do it Lord," My soul says, "Yes Lord, I am ready." I know I said this when I finally got it, but I say to you, "Wait a minute, cowboy," you have to be powered up first. God has an appointed time for each of his vision folk to be powered up before its show time.

I explain it like a Christmas tree effect. Nobody (at least, I don't) sits around their Christmas tree "Oohh aah-h"ing before you turn on the tree lights you fought hours to string around it. This might sound totally lame, but I think there is something so magical about the moment when you turn on all the wonderful Christmas tree lights.

Each year, my family Christmas tree is different. Before my daughter got her own house, she would decorate the Christmas tree, and then later my husband and I took over the responsibility. Regardless, there is still that moment when you turn off all the other lights in the room, and with excited anticipation, power up your tree. The electricity hits it and boom, it's Christmas! As Christians, I think God transforms us from what we were by salvation and then, at the right moment, powers us up to be magnificent for his glory and purpose.

Let me give you another visual because I live in Pittsburgh and think about this every time I see our big Light Up Night event. Because this event reminds me of what God does in us when we decide to pay the cost. The Annual Light Up Night for the citizens of Pittsburgh is a fantastic night out with family and friends that includes all types of fun events, music and food. For us, the police and other public safety personnel, not so much.

Anyway, in the center of town, the city places a huge Christmas tree-like structure. The city officials spend a good deal of money and time prior to this event by placing all sorts of lights and decorations on this large tree. Now I watch this process as I go about my business going to and from court, etc. However, until the designated time and date, that huge tree sits dark but fully decorated, with all of its necessary elements needed to be awesome for the Light Up Night event. Like Christians, the huge Christmas tree went through all the required transformations, but it's in a holding pattern until its appointed time to be powered up and boom, its show time.

Like the tree in my story, we all have some decoration we were born with and then more is added to us, as we grow in Christ. However, sometimes we are placed in a holding pattern waiting for God's appointed time to be powered up. The day we accepted Christ as our Savior, we were repositioned and reconnected with God. We are spiritually born-again; we are new creatures in Christ Jesus. Everything you need, God either deposited in you by spiritual growth or some things were placed in you from birth. The only thing that is needed is the correct power source to activate it all. I think teachers, leaders, and heroes are born every day. They are ordinary people who received the right spark that cause their natural born gifts to grow. God knows who will accept Christ and whose names will never be written in the book of life. Some of our names are in this book of life, we have salvation, but we sit dormant, existing in life without ever allowing God to power us up. In this state, some believers give up and backslide.

Back to the story, at the climax of this Light Up Night event, Santa walks out onto a tall stage located about 300 feet directly across from the huge Christmas tree.

The entire crowd goes wild. All of the children are simply awestruck at the sight unfolding in front of them. The crowd and the announcer begin the countdown: "Ten, nine, eight, seven," and so on. When the crowd gets to one, Santa takes what looks like a glowing sparkling snowball and throws it across the entire crowd to the awaiting tree. *Boom*, the sparkle ball/light hit the tree, and instantly, the once dull tree is fantastic and brilliant. Even this fifty-two-year-old woman's heart jumps for joy a little. Okay, I admit it—a lot.

This is exactly what God does in us. That anticipation, that restlessness you might be feeling is because you are being transformed; you are in countdown mode. God is preparing to throw the power switch in your life. Every cell in your body stands ready, for God to say, "NOW"- its show time.

UNDERSTANDING:

For me, once I was powered up, it was like cogs of a wheel clicking into place. I gained understanding and began to move forward. Remember, everybody's pace is different. As I look over my life, I came to understand some of the worst times in my life were the times when God was in the process of placing extra decorations on me so in his designated time, I would sparkle brighter and be more brilliant and effective.

That's my life in a nutshell. Once you gain under-standing of your God designed destination and submit to the countdown process, God will power you up. Things will, at times, get harder and come at you fast but remember God is with you during your entire count down process, God is preparing you for your appointed time. In this countdown phase, you might be tempted to think maybe God has forgotten about you or maybe you got it all wrong. Periodic inventory of your spiritual self will help to keep you from deviating from the path God has chosen for you. However, once you do an inventory of your soul and you are confident God is first in your life, you must decide **to maintain your position**. Press into the process even more than before by reading, praying, and worshiping God because breakthrough is close. Don't get discouraged when all your efforts of doing things the right way, don't seem to make a difference. They do. At times during your process God will put you in a holding pattern; much like a jet airplane circling around, until the pilots gets the okay from the Tower to land. During the holding patterns of my life, is when I have found, God is developing my spiritual muscles.. God prepared me spiritually to be able to run the race he destined for me to travel. When I lift weights, I do not move to a heavier weight until I master the weight that I am at first. I cannot move to a heavier weight until my muscle is strong enough to bear the extra burden of the heavier weight. The end result of this process is a stronger, better-developed muscle. God develops our spiritual muscles in much of the same way through the power of his Holy Spirit.

"Then he said to me, "This is what the Lord says to Zerubbabel: It is not by force nor by strength, but by my Spirit, says the Lord Almighty." -Zechariah 4:6

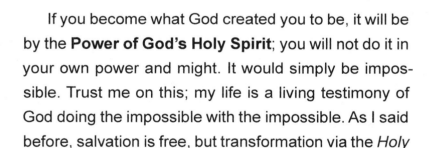

If you become what God created you to be, it will be by the **Power of God's Holy Spirit**; you will not do it in your own power and might. It would simply be impossible. Trust me on this; my life is a living testimony of God doing the impossible with the impossible. As I said before, salvation is free, but transformation via the *Holy Spirit* will cost you.

God's Word was not only talking to Zechariah here; he is talking to us now. Zechariah predicted more about our Lord Jesus Christ coming than any other Old Testament prophet, except Isaiah. If you read the Old Testament, it is all about the coming of our Messiah (Jesus Christ). Make no mistake—Jesus is the Lord of the armies of heaven. The Holy Spirit is the power by which God operates.

Just as the number one comes before the number two, so shall your transformation process proceed. God is an orderly God, so he will never jump you from step one to step three; you must be transformed in order, from one to two to three to four. There is no way around this; you must go directly through it.

This transforming process is different for everybody. The time it takes to move through your steps depends on many factors we will discuss in this book. I pray in Jesus' name it does not take you as long as it took me to go from step to step. From growth to growth. From milk to meat.

CHAPTER 5:

JUMPED IN

I was saved (born-again) when I was nineteen years old. However, I did not gain any understanding about God's will for my life until I was forty-five. At the age of fifty is when I was powered up. The Gospel of Jesus Christ was brought to me by one of my best childhood friends. We reconnected with each other once I returned home (almost age eighteen) from my time as a runaway. I ran away from home when I was sixteen and lived in various places and flophouses with an evil physically abusive man. This man (I will not use his name) will be known by what he was, an evil man, who was thirteen years older than me. My friend who I reconnected with was a bisexual woman who had found Christ. She was still bisexual, but had shouldered her cross and followed Christ. She would, however, throughout her entire life, wrestle with this particular sin. To God sin is sin, and we *all* have sin. God went to the cross for everybody.

I ran away from home with this evil man after my sixteenth birthday. One day while my mother was at work and Ethan at school, I left my family, my friends, and my school to go with a man who drove a beat up old truck; he had borrowed from a friend. This evil man convinced my young foolish self that my mother's house was not a place that I needed to be anymore. So we packed my stuff up and left. My dear mother had no idea where I was for almost two years. As a mother and grandmother now, I can't imagine the pain and sorrow I caused her by running away from home. My mother, who I respect and love to no end, had during this period of my life, a horrible relationship.

At sixteen, I was a confused, mean, angry child who knew nothing about the things of God. I was the definition of a heathen. I had so much anger and stubbornness in my heart. I don't know what my mother could have done differently to help me. My mother was never a touchy feely person; she had many issues that began in her childhood. As a child, my mother was never loved and cared for properly. My mother is one of the strongest people I know. She survived a life of neglect and abandonment by her mother by only the grace of God. Some of the things my mother told me that she and her siblings went through were not only a sin, but literally a crime. As a child abuse detective, I have seen the damage people can do to their children, if they neglect their duties as a parent. Anytime a parent prefers being in a bar or pursuing a social life over providing the basic necessities, like food and shelter for their child, it can become a stronghold for that child/adult and a generation curse for the child's future generations.

My mother would tell me stories on how she and her younger brothers and sister lived in one room and did not see their mother for days. My mom had two younger brothers and one younger sister, and basically she became the mother they did not have at a ridiculously young age. My mother would make sure everybody got to school. Their clothes were old, but my mom kept them clean. My mother said when it came time for lunch at school they would go in the back allies in Braddock and hide and wait until lunch was over because they were embarrassed they had no food to eat. My mother learned early to depend on nobody. A child who does not have a childhood is often not a touchy feely type of person.

In order for my mother to survive in her everyday life, she developed a spirit of pride and stubbornness. Pride in my mother was not the pride that says, "I am better than you" type of pride. No, another form of this spirit of pride comes in the form of "I do not need or want anyone's help." Because the people who were supposed to build trust in her character did not, she learned to harden her heart to avoid getting hurt again and again. My mother accomplished so much in her life. She put herself through school by day and worked nights to eventually become a Registered Nurse. She is currently eighty-three years old and does crossword puzzles with a pen. We both have grown and currently have a loving relationship. I think God provided me with the right mom so I could be exactly who he created me to be. Sometimes even what looks like to be the worst plan is still God's plan.

So let me give you the full picture. Like a lot of us, I was born into this world with generational strongholds from both parents. Add to this the trauma that sexual abuse can cause and the usual normal teenage drama and you get an angry and rebellious child. I don't have strong memories of my sexual abuse. I have small snapshots here and there of various events that occurred long ago. God has so completely healed and delivered me from all of my past; these snapshots are a distant memory that has totally lost its sting. Then, however, was a different story. If God had not intervened in my life, I am sure I would be dead or in jail by now. Rage and torment was my name. Even in this time of my life, God used a horrible thing to shape and mold me for later. All things do work for the good of those who are called according to his purposes. God at no time wants a child to be assaulted in any form, but it happens; we live in a dark and fallen world. As strange as it sounds, I believe I am a good sexual assault detective because I have walked in my victims' shoes.

Many of the events that occurred with me during the time I was on the run, I have put far back in my mind until God called me to write this book. During the time I was a Runaway, I lived a lifetime of experiences. The evil man, who I ran away with turned out to be very abusive. On one occasion, when I would not do what he wanted me to do, he threw me down a flight of steps. My body fell into a glass shelf at the bottom of the steps, located in the dank, smelly, roach and spider-infested basement. This basement was located in a person's home that I did not know. Somehow, the evil man had convinced these people to let us flop in their home for a few days. I remember cleaning the house while the owners of the home were at work, as sort of payment for living there. This guy and his wife, in fact, the entire family, were large, morbidly obese people whose toilet would often back up into the basement, where we slept. As I write this, I swear I can faintly recall the terrible smell this caused.

The first time the evil man threw me down the steps; I flew from the top of the steps to the cement floor at the bottom of the steps. The force of my body hitting the floor totally shattered a glass table located at the bottom of the steps. The impact of my fall knocked me silly and knocked the wind out of my body. I could not get up right away, so I laid there face down on the floor. As this evil man stood over the top of my body he purposely stepped on one of my legs. The weight from his body broke my toe and caused my thigh to be pressed into the shattered glass. This caused blood to be everywhere and literally a chunk of my thigh was gauged out by the piece of shattered glass.

This man was sadistic; there would be no hospital for my injuries; they healed on their own. I had an ugly permanent scar on my leg until a plastic surgeon, at the age of forty, filled it in with fat from other areas of my body. I have no traces on my leg from this event, but my toes and right foot still give me pain every now and then.

I believe God took me out of this situation because this man would have eventually killed me. I remember prior to my rescue, the evil man choked me with his bare hands to the point I felt my hyoid bone in my throat bend, but by the grace of God, not break. I was passing out. I guess he thought I was dead, so he released his grip, which allowed my bone in my throat to snap back up. As I write this, I still can feel this horrifying experience, and it still makes me shiver. I do believe alcohol influenced this man's behavior, but mostly it was because he was a dark person. By chance, a few years ago, I was talking to an old friend who mentioned he had heard, a few years back, the evil man had been working on a gas oven and it blew up in his face. I forgave this evil man long ago, but at the same time, I can't say I was upset to hear this had occurred.

I write about these events about my domestic abuse to possibly encourage a reader who is currently trapped in a similar situation or recovering from one. It is a good possibility a person such as this could read this book. One out of every four women and one out of every six men have been in some type of sexually or physically abusive relationship. Note: There is confidential help: (412) 687-8005 ext. #1. They will direct you to help no matter where you're located. Remember God is and was faithful to me, even when I had no idea who he was.

"I knew you before I formed you in your mother's womb. Before you were born I set you apart and appointed you as my spokesman to the world."
–Jeremiah 1:5

God might not appoint you to be a prophet to the nations, but I promise you he knows you and there is a purpose and mission for your life.

After the choking event, I broke down and called my mother (like the prodigal son) and we talked, but I don't think at the time I was ready to come home. Ready to admit she was right and I had failed in ways she could never imagine. Hard to see the logic in it now, but I inherited the spirit of pride from my mother (sad but true). Somehow in one of these conversations, I spoke with my brother who at the time was thirteen years old. My brother Ethan and I were close, and he told me he missed me and wanted to see me. I thought he would ask my dad to drive him to where I told him I was staying. To my surprise, one day I opened the door to the new flop house the evil man and I lived in, and there stood (alone) my brother.

Ethan, at the age of thirteen, had decided to get on his orange and black Huffy bike equipped only with Sissy bars and Banana seat and rode thirty miles to my place. Now, let me give you a picture of what this involved. Ethan and my mom lived in the suburbs of North Versailles. North Versailles is forty-minutes (drive) from downtown Pittsburgh. North Versailles, at the time, had few sidewalks and the main highway (the notorious Route 30) to Pittsburgh, had claimed many lives of people, some of which I knew. Route 30 is a dangerous four-lane highway, with no type of barrier in between the lanes. Of course, nobody follows the speed limit and it was common for vehicles to travel eighty or ninety miles per hour. Obviously this was no place for a thirteen year old to ride a bike. Yet, my brother did and just to see me.

Ethan rode straight down Route 30 to Penn Avenue, which will take you all the way into the heart of the city of Pittsburgh. This must've been a sight to see, because my brother was small for his age and did not start his growth spurt until eighteen.

When I saw my brother, I was overtaken with joy. Ethan told me he was a little afraid, but he kept pedaling. Ethan said he remembered where the statue of the solider was from being out and about with dad. Ethan told me, Mom did not know he had pedaled his bike to see me. This famous large statue of a soldier (named the Dough Boy) had been placed many years ago, at the point where Lawrenceville began. The statue was often a landmark Pittsburghers would give to visitors because it divided Penn Avenue and Butler Street, two of the main streets of Pittsburgh.

At the time I lived there, most businesses had left and the buildings were abandoned. Slum lords then bought some of these abandoned buildings and rented out the tiny rooms, to people like the evil man and me. I think we paid rent every week, so the lease was week to week. The evil man would do illegal activity or work as a day laborer to pay the rent. The bottom floor of this building was an office, so to speak, where people could seek work for the day without any questions asked. A lot of homeless men and women were in and out of this place. The area in itself was not safe to live in, especially at night. The upstairs of this building had one large room located in the front of the building; two total drunk guys lived there. These men would often expose themselves as they urinated everywhere in the building. In the middle room, there lived a woman and a man who I will talk about later. She was a prostitute and her boyfriend was not her pimp. Then the evil man and I lived in the rear bedroom that, unlike the other rooms, had another room we used as a kitchen. I considered myself lucky for the two rooms. I finally had something and somewhere that was kind of my own. I learned to cook on this tiny stove/ hot plate. Any of the food the evil man and I obtained, we got by stealing from the food markets in the Strip District. Ethan coming to see me this day, would not be the last time, he would unknowingly be the catalyst that began a series of events that would change my life forever.

Earlier, I said I thought God used my sexual abuse to benefit my sex assault victims. I feel God used this chapter in my life, to help others who have become victims of a violent crime. One of the common triggers for a domestic violence episode to occur is when the aggressor, the captor, feels like he/she is losing control of their victim.

After Ethan left to go home that day, the evil man absolutely hated that I had a person who loved me and made me feel like I belonged to something other than him. This evil man let me know he was angry as he always had—with violence. He hated that Ethan's visit gave me hope and confidence in my future and myself. When light starts to clear away the darkness (just as God's light does), you start to see the truth about the person and/or situation. For an abusive person, hope and truth are not allowed.

As a side note, any relationship you intend to pursue should always build you up. Run away from any relationship that does the opposite. A husband should make the wife a better person and the wife should make the husband a better person. Iron sharpens iron. It is even more important to be evenly yoked with the person than physical looks. Isolation and control are two of the biggest weapons an abusive person utilizes in their arsenal of darkness.

Isolation from family or friends is a sure signal there is a problem. Since abusive people are broken themselves (without help), they will never know how to love you correctly. For those who grew up in this type of environment, don't allow the very thing you said you would never do to dwell with you. Sometimes even the worst things become acceptable to you, if it's familiar ground. Abusive people want to possess everything you have, including the air you breathe. Never get this twisted with love—it is the exact opposite. You must always keep people around you who will be honest with you;

sometimes you do not see the wolves that exist under the sheep's clothing.

Back to my story, shortly after my brother left, the evil man and I had the worst fight ever. It was at that moment, I had enough, I was done; done with being stomped and punched to the ground. As I laid on the floor from what I knew would be the last time this man would ever beat me down, I saw a knife sitting on the kitchen sink. After watching this evil man go to sleep, I went to get the knife and stood over top of him, with every intention of killing this evil man. I remember the radio was playing Luther Vandross's song, "A House is Not a Home." I truly hate that song every time I hear it because it reminds me of this day. Imagine if God had not stepped in here; I would be writing a different book from prison. Instead the God, I did not know still lovingly pursued and kept me.

Every ounce of pride left me as the night turned into day, I was done here. I called my dad after the evil man left, from the pay phone outside my building. My dad, to my surprise, did not say, "I told you so;" he did not ask me any questions. I said, "Daddy I need to come home." My dad in an instant said, "I will come get you now, but if you go back again, I will not come get you ever again."

My dad was an old school cop. He knew this guy was bad news, so he gathered up a few of his work buddies, and trust me when I say they came into this building in full force. That's all I will say about this. Bottom line: the evil man let me go without incident. I went back to live with my mother. My dad brought me a long, warm winter coat with a fur hood because I literally had nothing. I loved that coat; it was expensive and I wore it until it fell apart.

Upon returning to live in my mother's house, I had to learn to live differently than how I had lived in the past. I did not know God; nor did I strive to know God. I still lived as a wild banshee. My mother was glad to have me home, but we still were distant with each other. Breaking your mother's heart can do that to a relationship. She never knew where or how I had lived. On many occasions she probably had dreams I was dead somewhere. My mother, to this day wears the spirit of worry well. So my running away from home must have driven her insane at times with worry. At no time did it ever cross my mind to return back to the evil man. Oftentimes, I would reflect about how my whole life could have been different, if the women in the middle room of the flophouse had not bonded with me. If my parents had known the things I did to survive, they would never believe it. I never prostituted my body, but it was probably only a matter of time before I did this also.

I think back about the couple who lived in the middle room of this flophouse. For the purposes of this book, I will call them Cammie and Stone. Cammie was a hooker, and Stone was her live-in boyfriend, not her pimp. Cammie was a small framed, dark complexioned black female. When she put on her wigs to go to work, to me she looked like a superstar. In the time I lived in this place, Cammie and I formed a strangely close bond. Even though she was not much older than I was, she became sort of a protective big sister to me. She knew I lived in a hellish relationship, and oftentimes I would hide in her one room so-called apartment. I guess she saw I had no idea about life on the streets and took pity on me. I think, however, she was put in my life by God to help me along in my process.

Cammie worked the streets like people work a normal nine to five job. She would come home and cook food on a hot plate that sat on the floor by the bed, which was also on the floor. The room they lived in was a small bedroom that never was intended to be an apartment. The bathroom was at the end of the hall, and we all shared it. From her, I learned to persevere even though you were dealt a bad hand in life. What I came to realize is I had it pretty good compared to where they both came from. Cammie and Stone appeared to have an okay relationship; I don't recall them ever arguing or fighting physically with each other. It was like all they had was each other. If one person were found dead in the streets, no one would miss them except the other person and me. The difference between you and them is you may go to an office to work and Cammie hit the streets to sell her body and

Stone hit the streets to hustle anything he could get his hands on to survive.

Cammie and I would have long conversations about everything. We both spoke about the ideal of one day having children. However, one thing we both understood is we would never subject a child to the life we were living now. Cammie taught me valuable lessons like how to cook on a hot plate successfully and use almost nothing to make crap food taste good. In this season of my life, I learned what it was to have nothing. Cammie appreciated she had a roof over her head, and she was partially proud she was independent, meaning she did not have a pimp. Cammie actually protected me from going into her lifestyle. She knew it was her lot in life but, somehow, knew I would be different. I appreciated her street wisdom because I had none. Never judge a book by its cover...God uses all types of people to mold us into our purpose.

Cammie's real life stories about the sex trade I never forgot. Thirty years later, my intimate knowledge in this area would help me to become a better police interviewer and interrogator. Like I said, never judge a book by its cover. A person whose heart is perverse and depraved can wear a three-piece suit and live in the suburbs. Who knew (only God) that Cammie's stories about her life would eventually have a helpful impact in my police career. I remember Cammie would tell me about her regulars, men from the suburbs who would search her out and pay good money to have her shove an apple in their anus. Yes, I said anus. Shocking then, but after working as a sex assault detective for twenty-seven years, Cammie's stories are quite tame in the perversity department. God made our bodies to have sex and to enjoy sex, only in his God-given parameters. However, there is no end to how Satan perverts the sexual desires of man.

Without God's intervention, man is lost eternally. We can be dark and depraved. I would have kept on this course except God designed a place, and time I would be introduced and exposed to the truth that Jesus saves, heals, and delivers. I had no idea at this time that this also included an abundant life in Jesus Christ. I know this without a doubt because my life is a living testimony that God does the unimaginable. In my pain and suffering, my transformation had begun.

"Now glory be to God! By his mighty power at work within us, he is able to accomplish infinitely more than we would ever dare to ask or hope. May he be given glory in the church and in Christ Jesus forever and ever through endless ages. Amen."
–Ephesians 3:20-21

CHAPTER 6:

A NEW THING

*W*hat I am sure of is God is doing a new thing. God is raising up a new army of people who are willing to step out on faith and trust God for the impossible. Spiritually, there has been a shift, and we are in the beginning of the outpour and the holy manifestations of God. It has begun. When God is making a move, it always begins with the church, his house. God will push out those who call themselves people of God, but bear no fruit in their soul, which is evidence of the *Holy Spirit*. God is making room for those who might, in the past, have been the people others considered on the bottom of the heap. I know because I was one of those people and to some, I still am. Possibly you know what I mean because you are the overlooked, the invisible. Well, get ready and brace yourself: *God anointed you*!

"I know all the things you do, that you are neither hot nor cold. I wish you were one or the other! But since you are lukewarm water, I will spit you out of my mouth!" –Revelation 3:15-16

As I look back, about fifteen years ago, God began a process in me that included a lot of painful moments, a lot of deliverance and healing from past hurts. I received many spankings; God only disciplines those who belong to him. Just as you would not discipline your coworker's children, God does not discipline those who are not chosen and called for his purpose. Understand God goes in order—one, two, three, four; he will *never* jump from step two to step four. So sit back and allow God to produce in you the fruits of patience and self-control. You *will* need to bear this fruit in order to be successful in your mission.

The stronger and closer your relationship is with Jesus, the more fruit you will bear. As you do this, the more power and authority God gives you. It's a serious privilege to be able to use the name of Jesus. Many people use "in the name of Jesus" in everything, but have never submitted themselves to the Lord for the fruit bearing process. Those people are doing lip ser-

"You did not choose me. "I chose you. I appointed you to go and produce fruit that will last, so that the Father will give you whatever you ask for, using my name." –John 15:16

vice; there is *no power* in their words. A **relationship** with **God** is what gives you the power and permission (authority) to use the mighty name of Jesus effectively. I have actually seen people use the name of the Lord as if it's magical. They think by saying—"In the name of Jesus" will get you your wish. Note: Jesus is not a genie in a bottle. Without a relationship with Jesus Christ, saying the words means nothing.

When God's fruit bearing process began for me, some fifteen years ago, I was in prayer, and the Holy Spirit pressed down upon my heart. God spoke to my soul and said quite unexpectedly, he would give me a new name. I have never told anybody this name (I won't say it here) because I was not given permission to share it. Therefore, it will remain personal and private. Perhaps we all have different names God knows us by. I don't know. I do remember reading in Genesis 32:25-28 Jacob's name was changed when he wrestled with an angel of God (perhaps Jesus). Remember Jesus has always existed; Jesus is God in the flesh.

One of the names of Jesus is Emanuel, which means "God with us." When Jesus appeared here on earth, he took a serious demotion. First, Jesus *decided* to be obedient to his Father's will and come to earth in the form of a human. Then, if that was not bad enough, he came to earth as a helpless baby, born into one of the most hated or misunderstood races. Remember what I said at the beginning of this chapter: when God is doing **something new,** he uses the least thought of by the world's standards and sometimes the despised. Jesus was definitely a new thing.

Our Father purposed our Lord Jesus to be born into a common carpenter's family; we all know the story. We celebrate Jesus' birth every year on December 25. Some experts feel Jesus was born in April, not December. They base these conclusions on information regarding the changing seasons and activities in the Bible. Personally, I'm just glad Jesus he was born. Jesus deserves to be honored and celebrated every day of the year.

Back to what I was saying—God changed Jacob's name to Israel, which means, "He fights" or "persist with God in prevailing prayer." Prevailing prayer (wrestling) is explained in the Word of God as being agonizing prayer, the type of prayer that involves (at least for me) a lot of tears, snot, and tissues. If you're going to dwell in the abundance of God and step toward your destination, then you will have to wrestle with God. It will cost you to be *transformed* into the person God anointed you to be.

"What this means is that those who become Christians become new persons. They are not the same anymore, for the old life is gone. A new life has begun!" –2 Corinthians 5:17

CHAPTER 7:

COCOON TO BUTTERFLY

*T*he fruit-bearing process is much like the caterpillar; it goes into a cocoon state and then comes out of this state as a beautiful butterfly. The creature is still the same creature DNA-wise, but it is truly totally different too because it has been transformed. When we accept Christ as our Lord and Savior, our basic DNA stays the same, but we are changed into new creatures. However, we must continually be transformed. Transformation is not a one-time thing; many Christians get this part wrong and fail to be all God called them to be. The transformation is a lifelong process, so you never arrive; you are always in the process of being transformed into a bigger, more brilliant butterfly. You are changed from a dead man walking to a person whose soul will never die; you will live forever with Jesus.

As I said in my earlier chapters, transformation is an uncomfortable process. I think of it like a pregnant woman who carries a child for nine months. She is expectant and excited about the new life she will bring forth into this world, but she is also apprehensive about the process called birth. The baby must also go through the necessary process to go from expectation to reality. There is no way around it—even with all the medical technology, cesareans, and epidurals. A process must occur before the baby is born into this world; it is the same with us, before we can walk in the blessing of God, we too must go through God's process.

My experience with the birthing process was much like my transformation in God: it hurt. It was uncomfortable. Even though my daughter was a total blessing from God, I did not like the process of pregnancy and birth. There, I said it; I did not like it and never saw that glow people talk about. However, I love the end result, which is my daughter. In both my birthing process and spiritual transformation, I tried to avoid the pain and sheer uncomfortable feeling. I was unsuccessful in doing both.

Spiritually, God was determined (thank God) that his way was best and his will would be done. Now the process was longer for me because God had to keep sending me back again and again through the process. The old folk saying is "a hard head makes for a soft behind." My head was hard. I had the "I'll do it my way" type of philosophy which slowed down God's transformation process in me, again and again. Eventually God would get his desired results but I was on the Potter's Wheel a lot! It's kind of ironic, but my attempting to avoid the pain of birth resulted in me sustaining lifelong medical complications because of two failed epidurals. Understand I am by no means against epidurals; I had to have two, and the second one helped me greatly. However, it was my avoidance and total self-absorption that caused me to demand relief for my pain. I knew once I gave birth, my daughter would be the only child I would have. Again in my, "I will have it my way" type of philosophy, I made the hasty decision to have my tubes tied shortly after the birth of my daughter. I often wonder if I was not a minority female on welfare as I was at the time, would the doctors have agreed to do this so soon. The truth is I would have fought until I got what I wanted—no more pain. Who knows what blessings I sealed off from myself by trying to avoid the pain of the process. I certainly didn't seek the counsel of wise men or, more importantly, God. I now know you have to be still and give God the space to be God. With that being said, giving birth to my daughter produced the second best thing that has ever happened to me: my daughter; the first being Jesus saving me.

The birthing process is a traumatic event to both the woman and baby. A nurse friend of mine told me the physical stress the baby goes through during birth is necessary. The birth process expels any remaining amniotic fluid left in the infant's lungs after its birth. So God uses a stressful event to produce life giving results; *amazing.*

Spiritual *Transformation*—is the process by which God moves you from a caterpillar to a butterfly. If you look at the outside of the cocoon, it looks like nothing is going on, but on the inside, all sorts of action is taking place. This process produces a creature that no longer slides on its belly, but has wings to fly. God is transforming us to creatures that soar.

I want to be clear: transformation can only occur when you have completed step one, which is accepting Jesus Christ as your savior. If you have not taken the time to say with your lips these words and believe in your heart, do it now and say: "I admit I am a sinner. I know sin separates me from God. Please Lord Jesus, forgive me now of all my sins. Help me, Jesus, to turn away from my sin. Jesus, please send your Holy Spirit to live in my heart and soul forever. Thank you, Lord, for your saving grace and mercy. Amen."

You might not have heard any trumpets, but *trust* all of heaven rejoices when a human being steps into the light.

Now we can proceed to step two, which is receiving the Holy Spirit. The Holy Spirit is a free gift that God has released to us the Body of Christ, but you still must *personally* receive him. The Holy Spirit is the breath of God—it powers you up to do the impossible. The Holy Spirit is the spark that gets the transformation process started. The Holy Spirit will lead and guide you through your transformation process also. The Holy Spirit is a gift from our God, our Holy Father and once you receive the Holy Spirit, he will never fail or forsaken you. The Holy Spirit's job is to transform you and to always give God glory. The Holy Spirit only tells you things God tells him to tell you. The greater your relationship with Jesus, the stronger your comforter, the Holy Spirit, becomes in you. If you do not regularly feed your Holy Spirit with prayer time with God and true worship, the Holy Spirit that dwells in you, will be ineffective and weak.

Again Jesus said, "Peace be with you! As the Father has sent me, I am sending you." And with that he breathed on them and said, "Receive the Holy Spirit." –*John 20:21-22*

In 1st Corinthians 2:14-16, the word of God tells us the Holy Spirit will help us to understand the things of God, but without the Holy Spirit's help the things of God will be foolish to us. Receiving the Holy Spirit means we receive power; we are powered up and energized. In Acts 1:4-5 **"Do not leave Jerusalem until the Father sends you what he promised."** Jesus told the group, "In a few days, you will be baptized with the Holy Spirit." They had to be powered up like the Christmas tree I explained in the earlier chapters. Jesus clearly tells them (Acts 1:8), **"The Holy Spirit will give you power to witnesses to people all over the earth."** We must realize it is in God's ability we rest and ride. The purpose of the Baptism of the Holy Spirit is *to* convict us of our sins and to equip and empower us for service

"As soon as they arrived, they prayed for these new Christians to receive the Holy Spirit. The Holy Spirit had not yet come upon any of them, for they had only been baptized in the name of the Lord Jesus. Then Peter and John laid their hands upon these believers, and they received the Holy Spirit."
—Acts 8: 15-17

The Word of God clearly points out a two-step process, which requires the person actively receiving the Holy Spirit through the laying on of hands after they have accepted Jesus Christ.

Without the Holy Spirit powering me in my life, I would not have been transformed into the person I have become. I can take *no* credit for it; it was done and is being continually done through the Holy Spirit. Again I say my life is a testimony to the existence of God and the power and grace of Jesus. With the Holy Spirit's help, generational baggage was broken over my life, as it will be in your life and our generations to come.

Through the power of the Holy Spirit, no matter what chains enslave you; lust, drugs, un-forgiveness, or bitterness can be loosened and broken in your life forever. I was truly in bondage and enslaved too many things. Some I was not responsible for and some I totally caused. Being in bondage is sort of like wearing five bulky winter coats at one time. Think about it: every movement you make, even the simplest ones, are exhausting. God works from the inside out (like the cocoon), aligning everything in your heart and spirit. I feel I look the same, but so many times people comment I look different than I used to look. So maybe there is somewhat of an outwardly change. People will say I look younger or something they can't put their finger on. I thank them, but I know it's the glory and light that only comes with a relationship with God.

A much older praying woman full of wisdom from Christ explained to me this effect. Embrace your light. Embrace reflecting the glory of God. No matter how dim it might become some days, it is still never to be hidden. I once met a nun who was so bright with God's glory; she truly lit up the entire room.

"You are the light of the world—like a city on a mountain, glowing in the night for all to see. Don't hide your light under a basket! Instead, put it on a stand and let it shine for all." –Matthew 5:14-15

Another thing the Holy Spirit does is he makes our hearts teachable and pliable for God's transformation process. I will tell you this story I often share with my teenagers in Bible study.

One day, I was in my kitchen preparing to cut my Fuji apple. It's the only apple I enjoy, so I eat them often. Because of this, I get pretty used to seeing what they look like on the inside and outside. I get my apples from a variety of stores, and I only pick the apples that look inviting on the outside. In my many years of eating apples, I have never come across an apple like this apple.

As I cut my apple in the usual manner, I reached down to take a bite, because I couldn't wait to indulge in the apple's sweet goodness. The anticipation is usually greatest when I am on a diet, and I have limited my cake intake. Anyway, there was nothing different about this apple; in fact, it looked the best out of the bunch sitting on my kitchen table.

As I went to place a piece of the cut apple into my mouth, I was horrified to see the apple was black and rotten in the center. I put the apple down because I was stunned. There was nothing I could see from examining the outside of the apple that would indicate it was bad. In fact, I saw no evidence of worm trauma to the skin or the surrounding flesh of the apple. The apple was rotting from the inside out, the rottenness was quickly infected the good part of the apple.

As I pondered this event, the Lord spoke to me through the Holy Spirit. Note: God speaks in all sorts of ways to different people; for me, it's not an audible voice, but it's a clear and different thought from my mind. I usually answer God audibly, as I did here. As you get closer to God, you will know the voice of God. We must remember God's voice will *always* line up with his written Word. It is *so* important to be filled with the Holy Spirit because he helps us interpret the Word of God and make good decisions. Back to the apple story: the Lord said,

"This is the heart of a person who refuses to allow my spirit to move in them; they rot from the inside out."

A heart that does not respond to God's light will not remain the same; it will, without a doubt, get harder and less pliable over time to the point the person (yes, a Christian) has no understanding of God. I have been there in my life, and truly you do stop hearing the voice of God; therefore, you lose direction.

"Their closed minds are full of darkness; they are far away from the life of God because they have shut their minds and hardened their hearts against him." –Ephesians 4:18

Living Life without God's direction, is like a person driving a car down the road without a steering wheel and hoping for the best.

God seeks a pliable heart.

"That is why the Holy Spirit says, "Today you must listen to his voice. Don't harden your hearts against him as Israel did when they rebelled, when they tested God's patience in the wilderness.
–Hebrews 3:7 (NLT)

A pliable heart is a teachable heart. A teachable heart means accepting discipline or redirection when there is a need to do so. A pliable heart is a courageous heart because change is not easy. It is the stepping away from old habits, some possible long-standing traditions and beliefs that may have been passed down from generation to generation. In some respects (at least for me), it was the stepping away from pride, stubbornness, low self-esteem, and fear. At times, I wore fear like a light spring coat that, over time became a heavy full-length winter parka.

Transformation is scary because it is the unknown; this is why Spiritual Transformation can only be completed in **the power of the Holy Spirit.** The good news is once you go through the first few stages of transformation you get stronger in your faith and trust in God. Over time, you will become fearless. Not only will you welcome challenges, but you will take a running start and leap head long into them. Practice putting to death all forms of worry and fear because you are free. Who the Lord has set free is truly free indeed.

When new challenges come my way, I do seek God first before jumping into it. Not all things are for you; stay in your lane and it's God who determines the lane you will run in. I have never been disappointed with the lane God placed me in to run. If you trust in God and leap, even with the hardest challenges, you will be successful. With God, all is possible. Here is what I have learned: if there are two roads, one easy and one hard, I beg you, choose the hard, most impossible one.

I said going through the various stages of transformation, the Holy Spirit will make you stronger, but it will also make your heart softer. Not weaker, but more pliable. Remember, a pliable heart is a teachable heart.

When I teach, I like to use illustrations and visual teaching tools to illustrate and convey the Word of God. I use the example of modeling clay when I explain the teachable heart to my students. Clay that is moist is pliable, moist clay is receptive to any type of manipulation from the artist. I show pliable clay, and then I show a piece of clay in the drying stage. Last, I show a piece of clay that has been placed in the oven and cooked to clay's most solid form.

The pliable heart will accept God's correction; it will humble itself to the Holy Sprit's leading and convictions.

It will allow you to absorb the light of Jesus Christ and then reflect that light and love back to others. God will press from the pliable heart any defect or blemish that could later destroy his finished product. Blemishes such as: hate, jealousy, un-forgiveness, pride, selfishness, and unbelief. As God kneads these blemishes out of you, this process can be uncomfortable and at times down right hurt. No matter how long you are a Christian, you must always pray to keep a pliable heart.

A heart that doesn't stay pliable and active in Christ becomes stagnate. A stale heart is much like a piece of clay that begins to dry out. There are still places in the stale heart that, from time to time, absorb some instruction/teaching from God. However, because the heart is stagnating, it rarely reflects the light and glory of God.

I find these Christians (and at one time, me) are the people who lose their way. They will say to me, "I don't understand the Bible; God's words don't apply to the real world." "Why pray, nothing ever happens. I also hear this excuse: "I would go to church more but my kids are involved in so many activities." Or, one that I used often, "I have a good relationship with God, I don't have to go to church." My favorite, which I have used in the past: "I am so busy; I am moving from the time my feet hit the floor in the morning; I have no time to pray or read the Bible." I warn you: be careful when you get into this area. I know because I have been here before.

Your decision-making will be off. Some of my worst life-changing mistakes occurred when my heart was in this stale state. Thank God our Lord is a forgiving God, and he allows us to have second chances.

A heart that is becoming hardened will find more things to place in front of God. Some reasons are valid and logical. Remember: God will not ever settle for second place.

"The Lord your God is a devouring fire, a jealous God." –Deuteronomy 4:24

The last stage is a totally hardened heart, much like a piece of clay fired into the oven. It is rock hard. For my class, I even tap it on the table. This piece of clay, much like a Christian's hardened heart, is formed into the shape that it will remain forever. This person is useless to God and his purpose.

This heart will no longer take in any light nor reflect any; it is not only stale, but it is dead. You will never be able to teach an old dog any new tricks. These are the Christians who no longer hear from God because the connection between them and God is stone cold. Their spirits have not been renewed or refreshed by the Holy

Spirit for years and years. These are the same people that sit on the front pews at church, but you never see them interacting with anyone in a loving way. I believe if this condition continues, you get what I explained earlier regarding my apple story: total rot from the inside out.

Bottom line: if you have the teachable, pliable heart, then you are in a position to watch God work miracles. The weight that once held you as a prisoner; un-forgiveness, worry, fear of failure—is removed to no longer weigh you down. Like a wine press squeezes the juice from the grape, so does God's Holy Spirit press your soul and heart. Good wine is the end result of grapes being pressed. When a Christian submits to the pressing of God, we produce spiritual fruit. Fruit of the Spirit is the gateway to abundant life.

CHAPTER 8:

FRUIT BEARERS

ow let's talk about the Fruit of the Spirit. The Holy Word of God often refers to the fruit of one's spirit. God speaks on your fruit being something that **remains** possible long after you're gone. Being a new grandmother, this is especially important to me. The way I see it is my future generations can benefit from the fruit I grow now.

"Ye have not chosen me, but I have chosen you, and ordained you, that ye should go and bring forth fruit, and that your fruit should remain: that whatsoever ye shall ask of the Father in my name, he may give it to you." –John 15:16

Now I think about our spiritual fruit operating much like how earthly fruit develops. You must first look at trees or the vines because they are the vehicles by which the fruit is brought forth. Usually a branch or vine has some sort of leaves on them, which bloom or grow every year. However, if the tree is not healthy, it does not produce fruit, and if by some miracle does produce fruit, the fruit is usually not good enough to eat. On the flip side, if you look at a healthy apple or orange tree, the fruit it produces rivals sugar itself.

"I am the true vine, and my Father is the gardener. He cuts off every branch that doesn't produce fruit, and he prunes the branches that do bear fruit so they will produce even more. You have already been pruned for greater fruitfulness by the message I have given you. Remain in me, and I will remain in you. For a branch cannot produce fruit if it is severed from the vine, and you cannot be fruitful apart from me." –John 15:1-4 (NLT)

I think Christians are like trees, we grow leaves because we are saved and reconnected to God. However, only with the proper diet of Jesus Christ, the Word of God, and prayer are we transformed into trees that bear fruit. As we submit ourselves and yield to the power of the Holy Spirit, you will produce or manifest the fruit of the spirit in your life. This fruit is so sweet and wonderful everyone around you benefits and (since it remains) so shall your generations be blessed.

As a Christian, and I am only talking to Christians here, once God calls you and you repeatedly refuse to submit yourself to his plan and process for your life, God stops calling. You are still saved, but you will never bear fruit. All Christians, as I said, will have leaves, but not all will bear fruit. God uses this illustration in Matthew for this reason; I do not feel Jesus was angry at the tree because he was hungry. Jesus never did anything just to do it. Jesus, like our Father God, always has a purpose for allowing or disallowing certain things in our life. It is our duty to simply *trust him.*

In the morning, as Jesus was returning to Jerusalem, he was hungry, and he noticed the fig tree beside the road. He went over to see if there were figs on it, but there were only leaves. Then he said to it, "May you never bear fruit again!" And immediately the fig tree withered up. –Matthew 21:18-19 (NLT)

Got leaves but no fruit?

The fruit of the spirit is the gauge that lets you know where you are in God's transformation process. The spiritual fruit is only produced in a person's life when we are obedient to the will of God. Much like gas is a byproduct of oil; spiritual fruit is the byproduct of submitting yourself to God's plan for your life. The Word of God explains it this way: the Holy Spirit produces this fruit in our lives.

"But when the Holy Spirit controls our lives, he will produce this kind of fruit in us: love, joy, peace, patience, kindness, goodness, faithfulness, gentleness, and self-control. Here there is no conflict with the law. Those who belong to Christ Jesus have nailed the passions and desires of their sinful nature to his cross and crucified them there. If we are living now by the Holy Spirit, let us follow the Holy Spirit's leading in every part of our lives."
—Galatians 5:22-25

The above reason is why all Christians are continually in a state of transformation. When you have the Fruit of the Spirit growing in your life, don't get comfortable or conceited because trust me, God will require more fruit. From fruit to more fruit to more abundant fruit, God is continually looking for people who will dedicate themselves for his purpose. This does not mean you sell your possessions and join a foreign mission (although he has called some to do that), but most likely God will call you to work exactly where he has planted you. A flower can grow anywhere as long as the soil is good.

The first attribute that God *must* develop in his servant is **love.** We get carried away with the word "love" and we misuse it. The love God needs to develop in us is the ultimate type of love—*agape* love. *Agape* love is unconditional love; love that is undeserved or unearned. Yes, as with all of the attributes of the Holy Spirit, all were first demonstrated by Jesus Christ himself. Jesus Christ never asks us to do something he has not done.

If you think about it, love is a weapon if utilized in a godly way. It was the unselfish love of God that blinded Satan to the wonderful plan of salvation. Now I don't know how space and time work in heaven, but I am sure Satan could never comprehend how such a powerful being like Jesus, could lower himself down to become a defenseless baby human. Love is not blind; evil is. Our Holy Father could have chosen Jesus to be born into a prestigious and powerful family. No, as usual God chose the least likely and most impossible circumstances for our Lord and Savior to enter this world. Jesus was obedient to our Father's plan out of love for us. Jesus knew from day one he was here to die for a people who cared nothing about him. Love was the reason Jesus spent a lifetime preaching and teaching the controversial word of God to first the Jews and then the Gentiles. Love is the reason why Jesus *allowed* himself to be murdered, even though he knew he had the power to activate heavenly armies to come to his defense. Jesus has always been God, and he has always been with our Holy Father. When he came to earth, he took a serious voluntary reduction in rank. Why? Because of love.

Satan could have never understood this type of love. How can anyone love a race that hates you? Love of people who illegally tried and convicted you as a criminal.

Love is patient and kind. Love is not jealous or boastful or proud or rude. Love does not demand its own way. Love is not irritable, and it keeps no record of when it has been wronged. It is never glad about injustice by rejoices whenever the truth wins out. Love never gives up, never loses faith, is always hopeful, and endures through every circumstance. Love will last forever, but prophecy and speaking in tongues and special knowledge will all disappear." –1 Corinthians 13:4-8

This type of love is hard and nearly impossible without the gift of spirit called *love*. Pray God blesses you with this fruit because love remains forever.

The world is always asking what love is and God clearly tells us what love is.

I recall many years ago, God gave me a lesson in the area of love. I worked for a boss who at the time was a good boss as far as his job went. However, his heart was full of pride and anger. He felt his anger was justified. Justified anger, if left unchecked goes into bitterness which caused an atmosphere of division and discord in the work place. One fly in the bottle of perfume can make the whole bottle of perfume stink. He stunk up the place.

On one occasion, I stood up for a person in the office who was on his "do not like" list and found myself on this same list. His anger was so ridiculous toward me, I tried on several occasions to talk to him and settle whatever matter he had against me. This did not work either; he outright told me to get out of his office. He wanted to leave things the way they were. From that time on, he refused to speak to me either verbally or in email. So I stopped trying and had to calm my own flesh toward him. It was at this point I had a tough time remembering God calls us to love the unlovable.

God reminded me that I (as his child) am still called to love those who are not all that lovable. God reminded me he is in charge and nothing can touch me without his permission. Remember with Job, Satan needed God's permission to touch Job and his family. Satan even had to follow the boundaries that God gave him to operate in. Sometimes bad things happen to press us closer into God. Over time, the Lord led me to write this same boss a letter of encouragement, which he did accept. Only God's influence in my life allowed me to do something like this after being (unjustly) stepped on by him.

The word of God says love does not keep a record of wrongs. God calls me and you to love those who are hard to love. Yes, we are called to still love the person who snatches the money out of your hand at the fast food place and then refuses to thank you for spending your money. Love is slow to anger.

Yes, we are called to love the person who you know to be Christians, but are downright mean and sharp-tongued to people all the time. I find God puts the prickliest, most difficult people around me maybe, to remind me what love is. As Christians, we all have to remember we should reflect or at least have a slight resemblance to the God we serve. My dad used to say, "You can't ride two horses with one butt." If you belong to God, obey God. God says love is patient and kind. Strive to be that.

CHAPTER 9:

JOY AND PEACE

*T*hese two ride together. God tells us not to rely on our own understanding. God further states in (John 14:27), **"And the peace I give isn't like the peace the world gives."** Peace is a gift from God, and if you have peace from God, then you will most certainly have the joy—supernatural joy that only comes from God.

There are many self-help books that encourage you to find your inner self, because only then will you have peace. In the past, I bought some of these books, which did give me things to ponder, but I did not gain peace or joy. We humans are seeking contentment and joy. We naturally crave these things because God created us to have this need. We have a need to fulfill this desire; we search for this filling in the same way we look for something to eat when we are hungry. People spend lifetimes searching to find that thing they hope, will bring them the peace and joy their souls long for.

Some of these books focus on the power of positive thinking, good karma, and even placing your furniture in a certain pattern in a room. There is no harm in reading these types of books and positive thinking is definitely better than negative thinking. However, none of the things I mentioned would bring you the joy and peace that God can bring.

In my career as a police officer, I have seen some positive thinking people totally lose their mind when life happens. Life will happen and it is cruel and unfair to many. Many times in my life, I would not have maintained any joy or peace of mind without God's supernatural intervention. There is one thing as sure as paying taxes: life will *always* seek to take your peace away. The only thing that stands in your way of your peace and joy is life circumstances.

I don't believe positive thinking would have helped years ago when I had to tell a family of seven that their mother was stabbed to death by their father. The ages of the children ranged from eighteen all the way down to seven. I can still hear the wails that came from the children as they realized what I said. There is a sound like no other sound I have heard that comes from a person when their soul has been totally broken. I know when I hear this sound and on a few occasions in my life, that sound came from me. Did I mention—life is unfair, unfeeling, and if you think for a moment you have manufactured enough positive energy to deal with the circumstances like this, you are fooling yourself. Only a relationship with Jesus will give you the strength and later the peace to survive this type of attack of life.

"If you do this, you will experience God's peace, which is far more wonderful than the human mind can understand. His peace will guard your hearts and minds as you live in Christ Jesus."
—Philippians 4:7

Attacks of life will attempt to steal your mind and frustrate your heart. Through Jesus Christ and the power of the Holy Spirit is the only way to acquire this type of peace and joy that will be able to guard your heart and mind. The world and/or your human mind will not be able to comprehend this type of peace, so don't try.

Earlier, I spoke about my brother Ethan being the catalyst for change in the early part of my life. Well, he was also the catalyst of change for me in 2013. This part of my book took me a long time to type; it's only been two years since my brother accidentally or intentionally shot himself in the head. One day he called me, and the next day he was gone, life happens. Ethan was a Christian who had leaves, but never bore fruit.

Ethan, as he grew older, let the bonds of alcohol entrap him, and after he was enslaved, the spirit of fear moved in and made a home in his soul. The fear of one thing grew into the fear of many things. Fear immobilized Ethan and caused him to refuse to ever travel the unknown, scary road. As fear took root in Ethan, it caused him to seek the comfort of booze to soothe his failures in life. I prayed for his transformation. In fact, five months before his death, a plan was set in motion for Ethan to leave his twenty-year destructive relationship with his common law wife and come and live with my husband and me. The last domestic fight Ethan had with this woman, she pushed him down a flight of steps, which caused an injury to his head that required staples. Yet, Ethan still returned to the same cycle of abuse because of his fear of change.

God, on so many occasions, used other people to warn Ethan to get off the path he was on. I spoke to Ethan on so many occasions advising him to submit to God's process, but fear kept him in bondage. In fact, in the last conversation my husband had with Ethan, my husband told him if he did not get out of his destructive household, he would die. I think sometimes as humans we hang on to situations and people long after their season has passed. Refusing to let go of what God has called dead will sometimes kill you. Shortly before his death and one of the last times I had coffee with Ethan, he told me his girlfriend was still angry with him because he had called 911 during their last domestic dispute. Ethan had people around him who loved him, yet fear enslaved him.

My brother was a catalyst of change, even in little areas of my life. In preparation of Ethan coming to live with us, we did a total revamp on our upstairs. My husband transformed a dusty old attic into a wonderful bedroom. This was a good place for him to live until he got a place of his own.

As the room was completed, Ethan kept putting off the time he would move into our home. Now moving in to our home meant he would not live as an alcoholic with any hope of ever working again. As God says, he who refuses to work shall not eat. Ethan would have had to begin to place one foot in front of the other and slowly begin to heal, which is a tough road many do not want to travel.

The bedroom renovations were completed in May 2013. My husband single-handedly did this work for my birthday present. We must have a decent marriage because we survived renovations. On July 29th at 3:15 a.m., my sister called me to say, "Ethan had been shot in the head and it does not look good." I was asleep so I missed the first call, so she left a voice message on my cell phone. I still have this message on my cell phone; I guess I keep it to remind me how God added the fruit of peace and joy to my spirit. In this time of my life, my sweet Jesus showed himself to me in the greatest of ways. I thought I had an understanding of God's power and love, but until this event, I actually did not. In this season of my life, God showed me how much he loved me.

"Don't be afraid, for I am with you. Do not be dismayed, for I am your God. I will strengthen you. I will help you. I will uphold you with my victorious right hand." –Isaiah 41:10

After hearing the message and talking briefly to my sister, I slowly pulled myself out of my bed to get dressed and get to the hospital. My entire body was numb. I can't say if I remember driving there or my husband taking me. All I know is I was soon there and walked through the sliding glass doors into the hospital emergency room, my body moved but I could not think; this entire event was so surreal. So many times I had been to this hospital, responding to a rape call out. I never imagined in my wildest nightmare that I would walk through these hospital doors for this reason.

The doors slid open and I slowly made my way back to my sister and her husband. I am not sure if Nate was there with me or not. That is strange as I am writing this because I do not remember. As I talked to my sister, the nurse walked up to us and I spontaneously asked her, "Could I see Ethan?" The nurse starred at me with a look of confusion on her face, but then must have realized I didn't know Ethan was already dead. In that moment, I knew Ethan was gone from this earth forever. No other words were needed.

At the hospital, the final conclusion was still the same as I rounded the corner and stepped into the hospital room. Ethan was dead. The nurses, who probably had seen their share of death, had prepared Ethan for us to see. Their kindness and thoughtfulness I will never forget. They had cleaned Ethan and the room up, which no doubt had his blood everywhere. The nurses attempted to prop Ethan up and wrap his head in some sort of gauze and close his eyes so he appeared to be asleep. I could not see any blood, but the irregular shape of his skull in the gauze was visible, which was a clear giveaway to me that most of the left side of Ethan's head was gone. I never touched him; I learned from my daddy's death. I cried some then, but the reality of loss wouldn't hit me until later. I guess for so many years, I was taught not to feel or act at that moment, so I tucked my emotions away until a later date.

My sister knew Ethan was gone when I got to the hospital, but could not stand to utter the words.

Ethan's common law partner had called my sister earlier that night right after the shooting. My sister and her husband rushed to the emergency room at the first hospital he was taken to because it was close to her and Ethan's house. He was already gone then and the doctor let her see him as he was. My sister has witnessed much pain in her life from a husband passing to Ethan, the brother she called her baby. She cared for Ethan (eight years younger) when he was an infant because my mother worked long hours to keep a roof over our heads.

June later described to me the events of that evening as told to her by Ethan's significant other. I feel I am blessed not to have witnessed Ethan's last few moments in this world. The scene, June said, was confusing with everybody running everywhere as Ethan was carried from the hallway where he was found to the ambulance outside. His significant other told June that Ethan went into the house for another beer, when he stopped to explain to one of his paramour's teenage family members all the benefit of going into the military.

From what my sister told me (and what I read in the police report later), Ethan tried to help. Apparently this teenager was scared to go into the military because he was afraid of guns. So Ethan retrieved his gun and unloaded it and gave it to the kid to hold as he told him how beneficial the military services were to him. Ethan took back the unloaded weapon from the kid and then put it to his head and stated there was nothing to be afraid of, pulled the trigger, shot himself in the head.

From what I am told, he either unknowingly or knowingly fed a bullet into the chamber, making the gun live. Ethan knew guns, but he was intoxicated. Guns and booze are never a good combination. Not only were we left with the horror of this event; we were also left with so many questions as to why this happened.

All at one time, I dealt with the death of my brother, his funeral arrangements, and my family's grief, while pushing for Ethan's autopsy and an investigation to be conducted. I called and spoke with everybody involved and not involved and still, questions remained. The end results of the autopsy are still listed with the manner of death as *undetermined*, and the cause of death as a gunshot wound to the head. As I said earlier, life is unfair, and serving God does not mean you always get all your questions answered.

Now in this devastating life-changing event (this may sound crazy), but God taught me joy. I still get emotional when writing about Ethan's death, yet I still have the joy only God gives. From Ethan's death, I truly learned what it means to enter into God's inner sanctuary. In his sanctuary, there is peace. In God's sanctuary, there is rest, and this is available to us *now*, not when we die. Our Holy Father, through our Lord Jesus Christ, allows us to come close to him. The Holy Spirit will minister to you and care for you.

One day as I sat alone in my bedroom before putting Ethan in the ground, the gravity of the situation hit me all at once. Ethan had sat at the county morgue for more than a week because his common law wife decided to keep the money that was raised for the funeral. Ethan had no life insurance and she had promised to give us this money to help with the funeral costs. It was a wicked time. She turned out to be in Ethan's death, even worse than she had been in his life. Every detail was a hassle, right down to getting the only suit that Ethan owned. The irony is she refused to give us the suit I had bought for him to wear to my wedding fifteen years ago.

The stress and the weight of this event on this day in my bedroom immobilized me. I had a breakdown and my soul broke. I made that sound I told you about earlier. It was now coming from my body. In the midst of my tears and totally separate from what my mind was doing came another sound: I prayed in tongues. I felt as though something prayed for me. It was the Holy Spirit ministering to me. I physically prayed, but the prayer was separate from my consciousness.

"Let love be your highest goal, but also desire the special abilities the Spirit gives, especially the gift of prophecy. For if your gift is the ability to speak in tongues, you will be talking to God but not to people, since they won't be able to understand you. You will be speaking by the power of the Spirit, but it will all be mysterious.

But one who prophesies is helping others grow in the Lord, encouraging and comforting them."
–1 Corinthians 14:1-3

I don't know how long this break in me occurred, but I know afterward, I was able to stand again. I could move forward again. The circumstances were the same, Ethan was still dead, but I could survive. My family would survive, and we would be blessed. Ethan's death was the catalyst for God to show me this side of him. Some of God's best lessons come to us through our greatest pain. I have heard people say this to me before, but before now, I never understood it. Also I never truly grasped how a person could be crushed and devastated, but still have joy. I did have joy. It's not joy like laughing, happy joy we experience when things are great. No, it's as solid as a rock holding you up because your knees are buckling kind of joy; it is a strong, rock-like, reassuring comfort.

I felt God's inner sanctuary. Hebrews 6:19-20 says, *"This confidence is like a strong and trustworthy anchor for our souls. It leads us through the curtain of heaven into God's inner sanctuary. Jesus has already gone in there for us. He has become our eternal High Priest in the line of Melchizedek."* This is for *everyone*. There is nothing special about me, and God is faithful to do this for everyone who submits to God for development.

Ethan's death also put to death *my* spirit of fear. I learned I rest in God's ability alone. I learned to *never* be afraid to leap and to utilize every talent God has placed into me. Before Ethan's death, I was afraid to do public speeches or teach. Even though I did it, the anxiety was so great that I did not enjoy teaching somebody something new. At times, I avoided it, and many times, I had failed. Many times my mind would go blank, which is terrifying in front of a lot of people. It still happens, and I am told it happens to the best teachers and preachers. I now roll right through it because I know God is with me.

We finally laid Ethan to rest on a Wednesday, but on the Sunday before that, my husband and I were scheduled to preside at the National Convention of the National Organization of Black Law Enforcement people. This meant we would stand in front of thousands of people, many of whom were police officers and high-ranking executives in law enforcement. The preparation for this event took two years of extensive planning. My husband and I were asked to preside for the huge Sunday event called the Blessing of the Badge.

Part of me wanted to run and crawl into a ball and mourn my brother, but God said no. In the midst of my devastation, God showed himself strong and his holy presence rested on this ceremony in a manner that had not been seen before or again. God put to death my spirit of fear with the death of Ethan, and again he was the catalyst of change.

Wednesday, we buried Ethan and again, God gave me the strength to be able to stand and speak again. In a little outdoor makeshift funeral home, which appeared to be a garage at one time, I spoke words a pastor might say if one were present for Ethan's final send off. It was how Ethan would have wanted it—only his close family gathered together one last time.

The same people who would have been at one of my backyard cookouts gathered around to say farewell to Ethan. As I looked at Ethan for the last time, he did not look like himself because he had been kept in the refrigerator so long. The funeral director, Ed, was a blessing and did a wonderful job. Ed gave everybody a clear warning not to touch him. I noticed flies began to gather around Ethan's head. Rich or poor, good or wicked, the flies will come and gather around all of us. I made a vow right then and there to utilize every ounce of the talent and gifts God placed in me for the glory of God's kingdom, while I am living; before it's too late and the flies start to circle around my head.

Fear can keep you from your destiny. Fear kept the Israelites wondering in the desert for forty years. Fear prevents you from the blessings God has for you *now*.

CHAPTER 10:

FORGIVENESS

*T*his one stands *alone*. Without acquiring this piece of the Fruit of the Spirit, you remain in bondage to your flesh. Forgiveness is for you, not the other person. Forgiveness does not come naturally to us as human beings, especially when our anger towards the person who hurt us is totally justified. It is beneficial to us to forgive, but I believe, at least with me, forgiveness would not be possible without Jesus Christ.

And then Peter came to him and asked, "Lord, how often should I forgive someone who sins against me? Seventy times?" "No!" Jesus replied, "seventy times seven! —Matthew 18:21-22 (NLT)

God calls us to forgive because *we are forgiven*. God gave His only Son (Jesus Christ) in order for our sins to be forgiven. The wages of sin is death, but because of our Savior's death and resurrection, we have eternal life with God. It cost Jesus dearly to go to the cross for you and me. So God does not for a minute expect you to refuse to forgive, no matter what horrible sins were committed against you. Our forgiveness from God is not deserved, so the people we must forgive do not have to be worthy of our forgiveness. You must forgive. It is not to benefit that person; it is to benefit you.

Jesus covers forgiving others so much in the Bible because it is *that* important.

In the scripture below, the King represents God, and in my opinion, moments after our death, everyone will have to stand in front of the ultimate King and account for their life. Now remember, I am talking to a Christian here; if you have accepted Jesus as your savior, then you have confessed and repented of your sins before God. In that same vein, you came into agreement Jesus Christ is Lord and the *only* Son of God, the only one capable of paying the price for *all* of your sins. So in this illustration, the servant owes the king 10,000 bags of gold coins. Today, one gold bullion (one ounce) of gold is worth $1,206.00. So can you imagine what the price tag on 10,000 bags (most likely not small bags) of gold is worth? Imagine how much those gold coins would be

For this reason, the Kingdom of Heaven can be compared to a king who decided to bring his accounts up to date with servants who had borrowed money from him. In the process, one of his debtors was brought in who owed him millions of dollars. He couldn't pay, so the king ordered that he, his wife, his children, and everything he had be sold to pay the debt. But the man fell down before the king and begged him, 'Oh, sir, be patient with me, and I will pay it all.' Then the king was filled with pity for him, and he released him and forgave his debt. "But when the man left the king, he went to a fellow servant who owed him a few thousand dollars. He grabbed him by the throat and demanded instant payment. His fellow servant fell down before him and begged for a little more time. 'Be patient and I will pay it,' he pleaded. But his creditor wouldn't wait. He had the man arrested and jailed until the debt could be paid in full. When some of the other servants saw this, they were very upset. They went to the king and told him what had happened. Then the king called in the man he had forgiven and said, 'You evil servant! I forgave you that tremendous debt because you pleaded with me. Shouldn't you have mercy on your fellow servant, just as I had mercy on you?' Then the angry king sent the man to prison until he had paid every penny. That's what my heavenly Father will do to you if you refuse to forgive your brothers and sisters in your heart."
–Matthew 18: 23-35 (NLT)

worth today. If it's anything like the old cowboy bags of gold in the movies, that's a lot of money the servant owed. Which brings me to another point: God's resources are unlimited. The king in this story (who represents God) decided one day to see what was going on with his servants. He did not start to settle his outstanding accounts because he was in need of anything. So, to all the Christians who do not tithe, God doesn't need your money; he uses tithes and offerings as an opportunity to bless us.

Anyway, back to the story. As Christians, our numerous past, present, and future sins are forgiven by the King/God. Through the death, rise, and rule of Jesus, our sin debt is totally forgiven. Done, paid in full, period. However, if we choose to live a life of failing to forgive others for many reasons such as, "That's the way God made me," or, "that's the way I am," then you are doing what the servant did to the guy who owed him silver, not gold, coins. The man wanted forgiveness, but he did not want to forgive. The debt owed to you is never, no matter what, more than the debt Jesus paid off for you. Remember, eternity is forever; that is what God gives you with him. Can you pay the going rate for eternity?

This story even goes a step further. This servant not only failed to forgive, but he wanted revenge. He used violence, which means his forgiveness had already moved past anger and right into hatred and rage. This tells me the man had a problem in this area already and probably spent a lifetime of not forgiving others. This servant's heart was dark and mostly full of pride. He was deaf to the pleas of his fellow servants' cries for mercy. In fact, the King called the servant wicked and then handed him over to be tortured. That handed over part does not sound good; it's a fate worse than death when the Lord takes his hands off of you. Sometimes, God does nothing to you; but leave you alone, which allows evil to do what evil does. Satan and his boys are quite good at their job. Satan's pleasure comes when he successfully moves a Christian out of God's Holy protection.

Because of my past, forgiveness did not come easy for me. I said forgiveness stood alone, but the spirit of un-forgiveness has many companions. I know I was intimately familiar with several of them. Their names are Anger, Hate, Bitterness, Rage, Rebellion, Guilt, Fear, Depression, and Despair. When you do not deal with an unforgiving spirit, you are rarely fruitful. This poison becomes a stronghold

"And do not bring sorrow to God's Holy Spirit by the way you live. Remember, he is the one who has identified you as his own, guaranteeing that you will be saved on the day of redemption. Get rid of all bitterness, rage, anger, harsh words, and slander, as well as all types of malicious behavior.
Instead, be kind to each other, tenderhearted. forgiving one another, just as God through Christ has forgiven you." –Ephesians 4:30-32

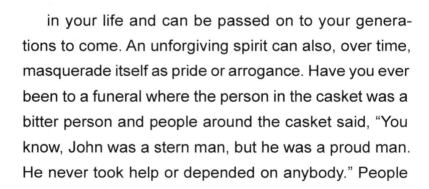

in your life and can be passed on to your generations to come. An unforgiving spirit can also, over time, masquerade itself as pride or arrogance. Have you ever been to a funeral where the person in the casket was a bitter person and people around the casket said, "You know, John was a stern man, but he was a proud man. He never took help or depended on anybody." People say that like it's a good thing.

Failure to forgive is responsible for many murders and aggravated assaults against other human beings. When you feel you have been done wrong, whether that injustice is real or in your mind, the response is often revenge and it is dangerous territory. I sat face to face with many people who appeared to live normal lives, but somewhere, somehow along the way, they allowed the spirit of un-forgiveness to take root in their hearts.

Many times, after revenge has had its way with you, the people find themselves sitting alone in the police interrogation room. I remember in one case, the man, in a fit of rage, took a hammer and beat his mate in the face into something that was unrecognizable as a human face. Because we are human we are born with emotions such as anger, but over time, evil takes a natural thing and obliterates or counterfeits its original purpose. Satan is great at changing something God gives us naturally into a perverse purpose.

Sex is a wonderful example of this; sex is a gift from God. However, evil destroys what should be a wonderful aspect of marriage. The sex industry is a multi-billion dollar industry.

Unfortunately, for twenty-seven years, I had a front row seat to experience the depravity and perversity of man. Satan will often overemphasize you are totally justified for refusing to forgive someone. Satan will whisper to you, "If God is really God, why would he allow this to happen to you?" Satan will regularly use a human emotion to ride on and exploit. How many times have you heard a person say, "I am a good person, so I am entitled to feel this way." Once again, from my experience, pride and arrogance will blind you and the spirit of un-forgiveness loves pride and arrogance. Evil is like a run in a pair of pantyhose—once there, the tear will get bigger and bigger. It's only a matter of time.

I often pray for my victims of child abuse because the hurt and anger toward their abuser is justified. This is one reason why these types of crimes are so horrendous—because they can destroy a victim over and over again throughout that child's life. People ask me so many times as a sexual assault detective, "How could God allow this to happen to innocent children?" Since I am one of those children, I can talk on this from a personal experience. We have lived in a fallen world ever since Adam and Eve messed it up for everyone, so life happens. However, God used my pain of the past to benefit his children in the future. I do not understand it, but I know I trust God in all he does.

"Trust in the Lord with all your heart; do not depend on your own understanding. Seek his will in all you do, and he will direct your paths."
–Proverbs 3:5-6

CHAPTER 11:

KINDNESS AND GOODNESS

*Y*ou can't have face time with Jesus without developing this piece of fruit. I dare to say if you don't see kindness and goodness manifest in the Christian's character, you know there is an issue. In today's world, this is not a trait recognized as powerful. However, remember this book is not for the world.

"Yes, I am the vine; and you are the branches. Those who remain in me, and I in them, will produce much fruit. For apart from me you can do nothing. Anyone who parts from me is thrown away like a useless branch and withers. Such branches are gathered into a pile to be burned. But if you stay joined to me and my words remain in you, you may ask any request you like, and it will be granted!" –John 15:5-7

A few years ago, I had the opportunity to go to one of the small islands in the Cayman Islands. It was a wonderful experience. The native people were kind and good; they believed strongly in Jesus Christ. The stores all had signs posted in the windows, informing their customers they were closed because it was Sunday and they were in church. The island was small and safe; nobody locked their doors. I saw women walking on the roads late at night. I was totally blown away by this because here in the USA, women spend a lot of their time looking over their shoulder. I spoke with some of the local police officers (who by the way never wore weapons) and learned that the last murder on this island, occurred over twenty years ago. This was hard for me to relate to because I feel I am always ready for something to happen. In the police department, they call it "Code Yellow." "Code Red" is what officers are in when involved in an active crime event. "Code Green" is what we should be in at home. However, this was the first time I had ever experienced Code Green outside my home environment.

One day, during this trip, my husband and I decided to take a drive to explore the island. I was glad my husband wanted to drive, because in the Cayman Island, they drive on the opposite side of the road, so the vehicle's steering wheels are on the opposite side too. The two-way roads were narrow and, in some places, barley paved. We drove for about twenty minutes, and the roadway went from being a barely paved to narrow dirt. This road led to some of the magnificent caves on the island.

We proceeded slowly on this narrow dirt road and I looked out the window and enjoyed the truly beautiful scenery, unlike anything I had ever seen before. The flowers were absolutely gorgeous; I do not have the words to describe the beauty of these flowers. The flowers I saw were a combination of purple, blue, red, yellow, and orange—all on the same flower. I am not a plant or flower person, but these flowers took my breath away. These flowers grew wild here; there was nobody around for miles who could have planted them. The beauty of the flowers was another example of the gorgeous things our God has created for our enjoyment.

That's where I should have left it, but I didn't. I knew these flowers had to have a name, so I thought it would be a good idea if I could pick a few of the flowers and take them back to our condo. I had all kind of things going through my mind; I thought maybe I could capture the flowers' beauty and find some way to plant the flowers back in the USA. As I reached my hand from the window, my husband stopped the car so I could grab a group of the flowers. The bouquet of flowers I managed to grab was on array of vibrant colors reds, purples, blues, and yellow. Satisfied with the flowers I now held my hand; I pulled my arm back into the vehicle and turned my head to excitedly show my husband what I picked. However, by the time I held the flowers up for him to see, no exaggeration, the flowers had lost all of their color and radiance and quite frankly they looked dead. This happened in a matter of seconds. I am over fifty years old, so it wasn't the first time I had held freshly picked flowers in my hands. I have never seen flowers die as quickly as these flowers did. I was shocked and attempted to explain what was going on to my husband. His concentration at the time was more on driving the difficult terrain and avoiding driving us off one of the many high cliffs of the island. His comment was short and simple: "You should have left it on the vine." Before I could say something I would have probably regretted later, God said to my heart, "He's right." The Holy Spirit brought back to my memory that his people are like those flowers. When we become detached from our vine, our source for everything which is our Lord Jesus Christ, we lose, even if we don't know right away, the thing that makes us truly beautiful and radiant.

Christians who stay connected to Jesus will produce kindness and goodness in their spirit. People who have acquired this gift of kindness and goodness are truly far more radiant and beautiful than all of the Cayman Island flowers put together.

The lack of kindness and goodness produces a condition called *self-absorption.* Self- absorption is the indifference to anyone's feelings or thoughts. I have seen cases where humans have watched another person suffer to the point of death right in front of them, but cannot tell you any details of the crime because they were on their cell phone absorbed in only themselves.

Next time you're in a restaurant, check out how many groups of people you see sitting together, but not interacting with each other. Watch: they do not look at each other; they sit together, but everybody is self-absorbed in their cell phone or some sort of computer device. It is not only young people. I have walked into homes to do an interview and the entire family is sitting in the kitchen, but they are all on their phones. Indifference and Self-absorption are worse than pride and arrogance in some respect, because indifference really does not care one way or the other and Self –absorption, doesn't care about anything but itself.

Over the years, I have watched the incidents of child abuse cases become so rampant the police investigators can barely keep up with all the cases. My facts don't come from a study that we, as the taxpayer, footed the bill to discover; no this is what I know to be true as a criminal investigator. Self-absorption is as bad as indifference. Self- absorption causes a mother to seek what they want before tending to the needs of their child. Having a baby is celebrated, but the work of caring for a child for the next eighteen years gets old quickly because of self-absorption.

I remember one case I had as a child abuse detective that epitomized self-absorption and indifference for me. Unfortunately, this was not the first case like this and it will not be my last. All through my career, God has whispered to my heart, "Go out on this case," or, "Pay closer attention to this or that." This was one of those cases. I was assigned a case early that day; I believe I was assigned the morning shift. I checked my mailbox and found the new case my sergeant had assigned to me. As far as I knew, it was one case out of about twenty; I would be assigned to that month.

I went to my desk and began to look over the report that had come from a child welfare agency. It appeared a police report was taken earlier by the Zone Police, and CYF (Children Youth and Families) had been notified. What I could not find was a record or a report to indicate where or what the condition was of the five children. If I can remember correctly, there were five children ranging in age of two months to ten years old. There were allegations of abuse from the various schools the older children attended.

The system for protecting children is so overwhelmed that sometimes there is a gap between the times the incident is reported to when it actually gets investigated.

The good news is, over the years, the police, courts, and child protection agencies have created laws and regulations that drastically reduce gaps in time, like this one, from happening.

Anyway, after reading all of the allegations, I was concerned for the safety of the children. I contacted CYF and was told a caseworker was assigned this case, but the mother had refused to cooperate with him. This mother had failed on many occasions to keep her appointment with the caseworker; therefore, he had not been able to check on the welfare of the children.

I hung up the phone and God said, "Go there now." I got another detective to go out with me, which was not easy when it's early and cold outside. As I gathered my stuff up to go to the detective's vehicle, I got a call from the caseworker assigned to the case. Apparently his supervisor had called him and he called me. I told the caseworker I wanted him to meet me at the house where this family supposedly resided. I needed to do a safety check on all the children. The caseworker told me he believed three of the children were in school because they ranged from five to ten years of age. However, the mother still had an infant and a three-year-old not in school and in her care.

As I tell this story, I can see God's hand more clearly. I have not thought about this case in years, so it must be the right time to tell it. We all arrived almost at the same time at the woman's house. The house itself was in a decent neighborhood. If you drove past this house in this neighborhood, you would never think anything criminal went on in this house. Child abuse is an equal opportunity crime. It crosses over all racial and economic barriers.

All three of us walked up to the house and knocked on the door. I could hear music playing and movement in the kitchen. However, nobody came to the door. I banged harder and more determined. The music went off, but still nobody came to the front door. I then got another strange feeling that made me more determined than ever. I felt in my soul somebody needed help. It had to be God speaking to my soul, because neither the other detective nor the caseworker felt as I did.

I had no warrant to get into this house, but I knew, come hell or high water, I would not go away. I needed to get in this house to check on the children. I yelled to whoever was on the other side of that door. I do not remember my exact words, but it was something like, "If this door does not open soon, I will open it permanently." The door opened. The woman who came to the door appeared to be a normal mom; she was a white female in her mid-forties with red hair. She introduced herself as the woman we wanted to see.

This woman appeared nervous. I knew something was wrong, but we could not figure out what. She made excuses as to why we could not do a safety check on her children who were not in school. She gave us bogus names as to who watched her kids, and when we said we would send a police unit to verify this, her story changed. I moved past her and said I would check the house to ascertain the whereabouts of the children. In this sort of circumstance, it is legal to do.

Everything in my soul said this was not good. I knew God had brought me here for a reason. I moved through the house with purpose. The home was a little sloppy, but it was not the worst I had seen. In the kitchen, the woman had a fresh pot of coffee brewing and a news-paper on the kitchen table. As we moved through the house, we heard no children, so we secured the woman in the kitchen because she still would not tell us where her children were.

I walked up the steps and saw several bedrooms with mattresses on the floor. No sheets on any of the beds. There were children's clothes all over the floor, some of which were stained with urine. I saw some chil-dren's toys, so I knew children did live here. As I went into another room, I saw a crib and a bare mattress with what appeared to be a doll lying in this crib. As I walked in the room and got closer to the crib, to my horror I realized the object in the crib was not a doll—it was a human baby. The baby was in a fetal position nude and wet with urine. The mattress was urine-soaked, so the child had been there for a while. The baby had to be cold because it was cold outside. The baby was so lethargic he did not acknowledge that I was near the crib. The baby was thin and small for its age, which we later found was nine months old.

I was filled with anger as I flashed back to the mother's hot pot of coffee brewing and the morning paper waiting for her on the kitchen table. I immediately found something to cover the child. I instructed the caseworker to come and care for the child as we went through the house to find the other children. I called for backup, and the caseworker called for more help also. I went to where the woman was detained and demanded in a not-so-nice way she would tell me where the other child was. The woman, we later found out, had no mental health issue, calmly pointed to the kitchen cupboards underneath the kitchen sink. We were all stunned, but after finding the baby upstairs, we did not ask for any further explanation.

Before I could get to the sink, other officers who had arrived on scene and had overheard my conversation with the mother were in the kitchen and pulled the four-year-old female out from underneath the sink. The mother stated she sometimes puts her daughter there to keep her quiet. I guess this helps her pay more attention to her morning paper. This pretty, blond-haired child was also lethargic and never made a sound. Being kept under a sink will do that to a child. After a short while, she smiled a little, but did not behave as a healthy toddler should.

As I walked through this house with the crime unit, they photographed everything and collected evidence. I then noticed a calendar posted proudly on the wall by the hallway next to the kitchen and as I read over it. I quickly realized the dates the mother had circled in red on this calendar indicated the days each of her children's social security and welfare checks arrived. We later found out this mother created the medical conditions in her children, which manifested themselves as medical disabilities. The mother then sought government money to care for the children. Once the children were removed from this woman's care, they all thrived both physically and mentally. All of these children were successfully adopted and are doing fine.

As I went back to where the mother was detained, I spoke with this mother who had no sense of guilt about anything. *Self-absorption* will blind you to think nothing is wrong with how you perceive the world. She had allowed her selfishness and greed to become so great she could not see there was anything wrong with what she had done. She was more upset she was not allowed to have her morning cup of coffee. I will never forget what she said when I informed her that she was arrested. I told her to stand up and put her hands behind her back and she did not want to at first, but later complied. What this woman said next has stuck with me always. The woman looked at all of us and said, "What about my needs? I have needs; what about me?" No concern about anything else. The only time a person so blinded with self-absorption and indifference gets upset is when the issue affects them. Yes, what grows in the place of *kindness* and *forgiveness* is frightening indeed. If left unchecked, this condition can be deadly. The world without the light of God is a dark and depraved place.

"...so that no one can speak a word of blame against you. You are to live clean, innocent lives as children of God in a dark world full of crooked and perverse people. Let your lives shine brightly before them." –Philippians 2:15

CHAPTER 12:

FAITHFULNESS AND GENTLENESS

*O*ur next two sweet morsels of the Spirit are *faith-fulness* and *gentleness*. Our very nature, our flesh, will always conflict with the Fruit of the Holy Spirit. In this day and time, being gentle is a sign of weakness. It is certainly not a typical characteristic police officers are told is in the top five characteristics necessary to be successful at this job. However, as one of the old timers at my job now, I would put faithfulness and gentleness as the top three qualities needed by anyone thinking about going into law enforcement. Faithfulness and gentleness for me, was only developed through a relationship with Jesus Christ through the power of the Holy Spirit. I am still growing in this area big time. To display a gentle spirit, you have to be willing to be a little vulnerable. This was quite dangerous for me, since I was hurt deeply as a child. Children who are victimized can take a position of strength and power to protect themselves from being victimized over and over. Some of the biggest bullies are the people who have been spiritually hurt the worst.

Without Jesus' intervention, I was a naturally harsh person, tough as stones, and relentless. It's amazing how God uses what you are to bring out your best. He uses what and who you are from birth to glorify his name. I think one of the most perfect examples in the Bible is Paul, or originally Saul. Think about it—Paul was a scholar of God's Word. He believed strongly in God and his laws. He felt Jesus was a direct violation of God and God's Word. Paul hunted down and killed Jews who accepted Jesus as their Lord and Savior. He was a smart, motivated, and a tough as nails kind of leader. Paul was beyond relentless at the job he thought was God's mission for him.

However, after a personal encounter with Jesus Christ while traveling on the road to Damascus, Saul, who was renamed Paul by God, did a 180-degree turn. The person who hated Jesus and his followers the most ended up loving Jesus the most. Paul truly did some awesome, unmatchable work for the Lord. God used the characteristic that made Paul such a horrible threat to Christians everywhere to become one of our greatest blessings. The Lord Jesus forgave Paul for all of his sins, just as he has with us, but Paul still paid a great cost for choosing to obey and follow Jesus. Paul saw the miracles of God, but he suffered greatly to complete his true mission from God.

Only a person born with great faith and the relentless iron will Paul had, would survive the many ordeals, he went through during his ministry. I think a lot of times, people ask Jesus to let them do miracles or be blessed beyond what they can imagine, but you must be willing to do the work, which will cost you.

God transforms us, but he also utilizes some of the characteristics you were born with to bring him glory. He redirects you on the right path and then poof, it's you upgraded to the tenth power.

This brings me to *faithfulness*. I have seen some of the darkest flesh-driven people demonstrate faithfulness. A gang member is faithful to the gang. An abused child is faithful to the parent who threw them in a tub of searing hot water because the child pooped their pants one too many times. A good man is faithful to his wife or his job.

The dictionary says faithfulness means you are reliable, trusted, full of faith, believing. The dictionary even uses Christians as a word describing us; we are called "the faithful." So the world identifies us as faithful. This is because faithfulness is another characteristic that describes God. Our God is the true definition of the word "faithfulness." This is why we must submit ourselves to the Holy Spirit so we too can become faithful. The dictionary says faithfulness means true to fact, a standard; reliable, trusted, or believed. Faithfulness describes the personality of God. This quality is so important; money cannot buy it. When true faithfulness is developed through the transformation of God's power, it's more precious than gold. Wisdom often rides with faithfulness, and wisdom is in great demand in the world today.

The world says everybody lies and nobody can be trusted. Well, I believe there is a standard; we as people of God must set the standard of faithfulness. When we speak as Christians, we should be able to be trusted and known as a faithful person. My dad would always say, "You can't ride two horses with one butt." Either your word is your bond or it is not.

Remember, God is *always* faithful. Even when we fall short of being faithful, God's nature is to be faithful.

The wages of sin is death. Nothing can change this fact. It won't matter you lived your life as a good person; if you are human, you have sinned. God won't change the rules no matter how unfair you think this might be. On the flip side, God is faithful; he promises you eternity if you do repent of your sins and accept his Son Jesus Christ as your Lord and Savior. Then, no matter the sin, you escape eternal death.

"God is not a man, that he should lie. He is not a human, that he should change his mind. Has he ever spoken and failed to act? Has he ever promised and not carried it through?" –Numbers 23:19

We can't comprehend God's ways of thinking with our human mind. God's way of thinking is so much higher and bigger than our human minds. I read somewhere there are twenty-one scriptures in the Bible on the subject of God's faithfulness. In my life, I've dealt with some smart people. Their minds are wonderful, but none can even begin to compare to God's intellect.

I remember doing an interview one day, and at the end of it, I came out of the interview room to discuss the interview with a prominent psychologist. This doctor had so many awards and certificates of achievements on his wall, I lost count. I began to explain to him how I got the person to open up to me. The person I interviewed was mentally delayed, and the psychologist was curious about how I broke the ice with this person. I began to explain to the psychologist that after the mentally challenged man initiated a conversation about God, we talked about my favorite subject, God. The psychologist then looked at me truly confused and said "Who?"

I said, "God."

More confusion, then crickets, crickets. Though this man had great intelligence, he truly could not grasp the concept of God. Possibly due to the fact, he had never felt it necessary to consider God for anything. I was stunned for a minute, because the psychologist still gazed at me with confusion. I then said to him, "God, you know, the boss of the universe."

He had no comment, but I quietly wonder to myself who was wiser; the psychologist or the mentally delayed guy.

Trusting God is faithful is a must, especially if you're a parent. If you have a child, then you must pray a lot. If you have an adult child with a child, then you know what fervent prayer is. The word of God is clear it says children are to honor and obey their parents. Adult children only have to honor us, not obey our every command. Until the Holy Spirit develops your faithfulness and gentleness, it is hard to understand God in this area. My job as a parent now is to give counsel (continuously) and give God room to operate in her life, as he did in mine. Easier said than done. As I wrote the beginning chapter on faithfulness, all hell broke out with my daughter to the point I questioned if this child had any common sense. Has anybody been there?

Now, of course, the moment I think this, the Holy Spirit flashes in my mind the many times I was stuck on stupid in my life. God reminded me my life is a testimony to his grace and power. I had to come to the understanding God is faithful enough to keep my daughter, my grandson, and generations to come just as he faithfully kept me. Satan will attack us in the area of faithfulness because faithfulness is simply trusting in the promises of God, regardless of the situations unfolding around you and your family. We must actively resist these attacks of the enemy.

"So humble yourselves before God. Resist the Devil, and he will flee from you." –James 4:7

<u>Gentleness</u>

When we are children, we behave childish because that's what we do as children. I was not born with a gentle spirit. Many children are not; this characteristic must be developed. Because of Adam's original sin, we are *all* born with a spirit that is bent away from God. This is why a child must have good adults in their life, which will stand in the gap for them in prayer and train them in the proper way to go. An adult, who has failed to develop a spirit of gentleness, is at best not a person who is not enjoyable to be around, and at worst, they become a person who manipulates and possibly victimizes others.

"Teach your children to choose the right path, and when they are older, they will remain upon it."
–Proverbs 22:6

Gentleness is a must for us Christians because we cannot bring salvation to the unsaved without it.

To gentleness, add respect; they ride together. Fire and brimstone philosophy does nothing to attract people to Jesus. I do not advocate compromising the Word of God at all; God's truth is real truth. But, we as Christians cannot deliver a message of God's forgiving love harshly. There is nobody who God has saved worthy of this wonderful gift of eternity with him. We all fall short of the glory of God. As I read through the Bible, there was not one time Jesus had to shout out disrespectfully to get his point across. Even when casting demons, he was respectful, calm, and in full control and full authority. We, as the people of God, *must* mimic this type of gentleness always.

"...gentleness and self-control. Here there is no conflict with the law." **–Galatians 5:23**

CHAPTER 13:

SELF-CONTROL

The dictionary states, self- control is control or restraint of one's self or one's actions, feelings, etc. There are senior citizens who have not yet learned the meaning of self-control. This is the last piece of the Fruit of the Spirit, and trust me—it does not happen with the process of aging. God says self-control is necessary to co-exist in the world.

"For the grace of God has been revealed, bringing salvation to all people. And we are instructed to turn from godless living and sinful pleasures. We should live in this evil world with self-control, right conduct, and devotion to God, while we look forward to that wonderful event when the glory of our great God and Savior, Jesus Christ, will be revealed." –Titus 2:11-13

I use to think self-control meant discipline in the bad sense of the word, but it does not. It is actually a gift from God. One day, while talking with my daughter, she said self-control is a necessity for a Christian to learn, because God wants to bless us abundantly. To my surprise, she had been listening. She went on to say sometimes, God has to hold back his blessings, because we are not ready to handle them yet. She said big blessings couldn't fit in a little container; she is truly my father's grandchild.

My daughter used her budget as an example. She said she submitted her spirit to the process of learning self-control in this area. She said, "If God can't trust me with one dollar, why would God give me $100?" Makes sense because as I go back over my life, I remember many times God wanted to bless me, but I was not ready. I thank God for his perfect "one, two, three, four" timing.

My first husband was a good man and a good husband. However, due to my lack of self-control in many areas of my life, I threw it all away and walked away from it all.

Self-control keeps you under the covering umbrella of God, and as my daughter put it, "God has some good stuff under that umbrella." This world, whether it is evil or fleshly, has many glittery attractions outside of the will of God. The gift of self-control is a must to keep in check such things like sex, booze, food, drugs, or whatever your idol is. Satan will often attack even the strongest Christians in these areas, because it moves you from underneath God's umbrella of protection. The greater the lack of self-control becomes, the wider the door opens. Satan looks for open doors in God's people because an open door is our permission for Satan to enter in and inflict our spirit. A Christian cannot be possessed, but we can be afflicted and tormented to the point that we have little or no mental and physical strength left. Self-control gives us healthy boundaries, protection, and the wisdom in every area of our lives.

"A person without self-control is as defenseless as a city with broken-down walls." –Proverbs 25:28

Great power comes with great responsibility. There is a worship song that asks God to enlarge our territories. In truth, God will not do this until you are ready to receive it properly. There is no way God, in his perfect wisdom, will increase your territories when you have no self-control over what you have now. One of the hardest elements to control for anybody is the tongue. Many Christians have self-control in all other areas of their life except here. So often we Christians will look at an alcoholic and say they are the sinners but have no control over the vile language that comes from her mouth.

SELF-CONTROL

"I made a covenant with my eyes not to look with lust upon a woman." —Job 31:1

Without God's gift of self-control, in time, a person will be overtaken by whatever threatens to enslave them. I have had a front row seat to see drugs, alcohol, and/or lust destroy many people. For me, self-control was only possible through the Holy Spirit and submission to Christ.

I routinely conduct post-conviction sex offender polygraph examinations. These types of polygraph examinations are court-ordered for any person who has been convicted of a serious sexual offense. Once the person is paroled or placed on probation, the court and treatment providers monitor their behavior. Since most of these folks will be living in our communities, it is important to have some type of system in place to maintain and monitor convicted sexual offenders' activities.

I have seen lust cause successful and rich men to lose everything. It starts small, but as it overtakes a soul, lust becomes perverted and deviant. A lot of the men

128

(and some women) truly understand they have allowed lust to destroy their own lives to the point they are now labeled (in most cases, rightfully so) a sex offender. Note: In my experience ninety percent of sex offenders also have an alcohol issue; it is usually not drugs.

Lack of self-control in one area will usually open the door to other areas of lack or loss of control. Once you have several open doors spiritually, then it becomes a stronghold in your spirit, and this can easily become a generational stronghold. Alcoholism runs in my family. Both brothers had problems with it, and I am on constant watch that I do not become enslaved in this area.

Understand I do not feel booze is wrong in itself, but I have seen too many issues with it not to tread lightly in this area. It is totally legal to do, but not all things are for everybody. Seventy percent of all the sexual assaults I have investigated, the victim and/or the suspect were highly intoxicated.

Even in the law enforcement community, booze is accepted. Cops have a high percentage of alcohol abuse. Alcohol becomes a legal, easily accessible way of stopping the dark images we see every day from replaying in our minds over and over again.

Twenty-two years ago, I remember being the new rookie detective in the sexual and child abuse office. One day, I walked into the bathroom and overheard someone crying softly in one of the bathroom stalls. My reaction was to freeze because I did not know if it was a good idea for me to interrupt their private moment. I wanted to ask if they were all right. Now that I think about it, this was a stupid question. Of course the person was not all right; they were in a bathroom sobbing. Before I could decide what to do, the bathroom stall door flung open and out walked, to my surprise, one of the top senior gold badge sex assault detectives.

I will not use her name because she is retired now, but trust me—she was good at her job and was well respected. I have modeled myself after her, and I still go into the police report achieves and read over some of her case files, which are truly impressive.

To say I was surprised to see her come out this bathroom is an understatement. Before I could ask her any questions, this senior gold badge detective looked at me square in my eye and said, "You'll see if you're here long enough." She then walked past me, stopping briefly at the sink to wipe her tears and nose with a tissue. She then left the bathroom; we never spoke about that again.

I am now the senior gold badge detective in my office and on many occasions, I have found myself many times to be the person in the bathroom stall crying about the devastation one person's lack of self-control caused for an innocent child. She was right; I do know now. The lack of self-control usually hurts more than the person it enslaves. Casualties of human self-control failure, is the six-year-old child who, during a forensic interview, struggles to explain how her adult uncle (who the family loved and trusted) forced her to have oral sex with him. Another example of a casualty of self-control human failure is the male who followed his girlfriend from the women's domestic violence shelter (I placed her in) to her grandmother's house and brutally murdered both my twenty-year-old victim and her grandmother.

One of the worst cases to me, which demonstrated full generational failure of self-control, lack of order, and evil in so many areas, was the man and the mother who raised the man who murdered three of my fellow Pittsburgh police officers.

It was April 4, 2009; I remember I was at the Toyota dealer to get my car inspected, and my husband, who at the time was a SWAT officer, called me to say he was called into work because they had an active shooter situation in Stanton Heights. I was surprised because Stanton Heights is one of our better neighborhoods in Pittsburgh. The next words my husband said felt like I was kicked in the stomach. He said two officers had already been killed. My God, two of my brothers in blue had been murdered, and now my husband rushed to this same scene.

I spoke calmly, but I was physically sick. The conversation was quick and matter of fact, almost like he said he was headed to the store to buy a loaf of bread or something. We said we loved each other and that was it, conversation done. It was possibly the last conversation we would ever have. It is at that moment you better know God, you better have a relationship with him, because there is nothing, and I mean nothing, any human can say or do for you in that moment. Your life, as you know it, could change forever. You know it's possible, because the families of the already dead officers' lives had changed forever.

I pulled the car over on West Liberty Avenue and began to cry out to God for the safe return of my husband and all the other police officers. The Holy Spirit whispered to my soul, "the prayers of a righteous man avail much." This is why it is so important to keep God's words close to your heart and study them often. So I prayed. Bear in mind, I am *only* righteous because of the price my Savior Jesus Christ paid for me. Knowing God is God of everything, I sought his help first, which is not an easy thing to do when terror is looking you in the face.

As the situation unfolded, I learned the names of the three officers who had been murdered. One of the fallen Officers, I had trained in the police academy many years earlier. I would later stand by the foot of his casket as an amour guard. The murders were senseless. The killer was angry with his mother, so he decided to shoot the first two police officers who walked through his front door. The officers responded to the 911 domestic calls his mother had placed. The shooter's mother was a woman totally obsessed with herself, and as this chaotic scene unfolded, she calmly stood in her garage smoking a cigarette. From the accounts of this event, the mother taunted the adult son like she had done for most of his life; she often called him a failure and told him he did not have the guts to do anything. Well, the son did something this day. He murdered Officer Sciullo, Officer Mayhle, and Officer Kelly.

I recall when my husband came home from this call many hours later. He was quiet and never said much about the incident. The only thing he eventually told me was how disturbing it was for him to see a Pittsburgh police officer lying on the ground in full uniform, without a recognizable head. The shooter had shot the officers point blank with shotguns. That day I saw my husband quietly take off his SWAT uniform at the front door. He gathered them up and went to the basement to wash his fellow officers' blood from his clothes and boots. Life happens.

It is popular to hate cops and securitize every move they make, even when they do their job lawfully. There are no doubt bad cops, racist cops—I have worked with a few. Those cops disgust the good cops because they are a disgrace to the badge and everything it stands for. To most of us, our badge stands for a symbol of safety, trustworthiness, faithfulness, truthfulness, and courage. What most people don't understand is most cops want to make a positive difference and do their job well and lawfully. We, as police officers, come in many colors, genders, and religious beliefs, and in our souls, live by this prayer:

A Policeman's Prayer

Lord, I ask for Courage; courage to face and conquer
my own fears
Courage to take me where others will not go.
I ask for strength;
Strength of body to protect others
Strength of spirit to lead others.
I ask for dedication;
Dedication to my job to do it well
Dedication to my community to keep it safe.
Give me, Lord, concern;
For all of those who trust me
And compassion for those who need me.
And, please, Lord throughout it all;
Be at my side.

Failure to allow the Holy Spirit to develop self-control in your soul, will rob you of the abundant life, God intended for you to live. The more we submit ourselves to God's process, the stronger our Holy Spirit becomes.

"A kingdom at war with itself will collapse. A home divided against itself is doomed." –Mark 3:24-27.

The only thing that can take down the strongman (Satan) is God. There is not a war in this area going on; Jesus Christ already has won everything for us. This is why we must keep God in front of us in everything, while we ride and rest in his victory. Read the end of the Bible (Revelation): we win!

I heard a pastor preach one time, and she said those who are called and saved by Jesus Christ are covered with his grace, until the Holy Spirit in us is strong enough to overtake that sin that enslaves us. Obeying God and his command for your life builds up your Holy Spirit. In the beginning of my journey, I twisted so many times and fell short of so many things, but God still loved me. Grace is an awesome thing; it truly is favor that you and I have done nothing to deserve.

Satan's job, if you read the above verse closely, is to rob you of what is rightfully yours in God. He will always be opposed to your light because your light is from God, and he opposes God. If Satan is not bothering you, watch out, because this means you are totally lukewarm and not a threat to his kingdom or you are in the wrong house all together. As the above Scripture says, if Satan opposed his own house, it would be weakened, divided, and it would fall even faster.

Satan is the author of self-centeredness; he will never do anything to hurt him. In Satan, there is no light, no love; in him, he is the darkest of the dark night. He is void of God. If Satan is not pricking your side, ask your-self why. Whose neighborhood is your house located?

Be encouraged also, once your house is guarded up with the fierce power of the Holy Spirit, reinforced daily with time spent in fellowship with God. Satan has a tough time of entering into your house and robbing you. When he does come to your door, Satan must wait, crouching at your door until you open it to give him a way in.

"You will be accepted if you respond in the right way. But if you refuse to respond correctly, then watch out! Sin is waiting to attack and destroy you, and you must subdue it." –Genesis 4:7

You do not have to stand by and allow Satan and his demons tie you up. You do not have to stay in bondage to that thing that causes you to stumble over and over again. People of God, stand up and *fight*! The Lord Jesus Christ has given us the authority and command to become the strong man.

"Put on all of God's armor so that you will be able to stand firm against all strategies and tricks of the Devil." –Ephesians 6:11

CHAPTER 14:

FIRST THING'S FIRST

*N*ow all of this is a process, and if you are on the right track, then you might be thinking, "Okay, it's time to run. I have submitted myself to God, and he has and is transforming me."

In fact, you may be well out of the cocoon state. However, you feel as if you are still in a holding pattern. "I see others taking off and doing all type of fantastic things, but what's up with me?"

"Be silent, and know that I am God! I will be honored by every nation. I will be honored throughout the world." –Psalm 46:10

I had to learn (not always easy) to be still while constantly moving toward the Lord. So take your eyes off of what God is doing in other people's lives.

Years ago, I tried my hand at growing tomatoes because I really like them. If I could find a way to incorporate tomatoes into every meal, I probably would. I like them so much I thought it would be cheaper if I grew my own. I believe if you are going to do something, do it one hundred percent; so I went out, bought the right starter plant, pots, and the best soil. I got steak tomato plants because the big steak tomatoes are simply wonderful on a BLT sandwich. I did research on the Internet and spoke to people, who I knew had successfully grown their own delicious tomatoes. I was ready and determined this process would work. As I went through the process of planting the tomatoes, I asked for God to bless the plants because I believe God should be first in the minor as well as the major matters of life.

I then placed the starter pots in a perfect location and watered them with every kind of plant nutrient I learned through my research would be beneficial. I then waited and waited some more. Nothing happened for a long time, and then finally they began to come up wonderfully, all except one plant. I treated all the plants the same, but could not figure out why one chose not to grow. All the plants continued to grow; all of the plants had the same water and sun. All the plants except the one got big enough for me to transplant outside. I still kept and cared for the lone plant still inside, but I saw no growth. The dirt looked the same as it did when I had first planted the seed.

On day, I went to check on the lone plant, still left in the house and I was blown away by what I saw. The plant had literally grown overnight. How does this happen—one day, it's barren, and the next day, there's life? The Holy Spirit brought back to my mind that all is possible (things big and small) with God. God reminded me it is in his timing, not ours. In his chosen season, he will call us out just as quickly. When it is time, God will say to you, "Now is the appointed time: grow." In the twinkling of an eye and in a flash, it will happen.

"Before the mountains were created, before you made the earth and the world, you are God, without beginning or end. You turn people back to dust, saying, 'Return to dust! For you, a thousand years are as yesterday! They are like a few hours!'"
–Psalm 90: 2-4

This plant ended up being the biggest and the best out of all my plants. This must have been a God lesson, because I have never been successful at growing anything since. My other plants died because I had placed them outside to soon; I felt they were ready. We had an unusually cold freeze one night that basically killed all of my outside tomato plants. My timing was off, but God's timing won't be.

God will not allow you to bloom before your time. God sees all; he knows all. God will keep you grounded in a holding pattern, sometimes for your own protection. God will sometimes keep you in what you may feel is a bad circumstance. However, God is only using this circumstance to allow you time to soak in all the necessary elements that you will need later to be the biggest and the best.

When trapped in a holding pattern or worse—trapped in a bad or stressful place—remember the story of Joseph in Genesis 41. Joseph's story is a good example of how God works in a person's life. Joseph was a man of God; he was called from a young age. However, it was a lifelong process how God equipped and trained Joseph to handle all the responsibility that came with the huge blessings God intended to give him. If God had not held up Joseph's blessing for the correct time, he would not have known how to behave with his future success, money, and power.

In Genesis 39, we learn Joseph was in prison for two years. The prisons then were dungeons, not the human-friendly prisons we have today. He was not only in a holding pattern—he was in a rather sucky place. He had been placed in this bad situation unjustly. Joseph had done nothing wrong. This is important; sometimes God does allow unjust things to happen to us. When, not if, this happens to you, we should follow Joseph's example. Joseph had a relationship with God and he (most likely) against his human understanding, still submitted himself to God's will. Joseph's submission—as will our submission to God's plan—produced much fruit for the glory of God. If you're still and trust God in your sucky place, he will show you awesome favor.

We know by reading about Joseph (Genesis 40:14) that he wanted to get out of prison. The cupbearer did not remember him and time passed, because it was not yet the Lord's appointed time.

"Pharaoh sent for Joseph at once, and he was brought hastily from the dungeon. After a quick shave and change of clothes, he went in and stood in Pharaoh's presence." –Genesis 41:14

Don't miss this: you must be ready when God calls you to go before the king. Joseph had no time to prepare spiritually. He was already prepared by daily face time with God. Joseph had been powered up when he was young and transformed into being a huge fruit bearer. Joseph was now ready when God said, "Now!" Literally in an instant, his world changed drastically. Be ready. Keep your head down and your eyes on your own paper. Press into your relationship with Jesus Christ; shortly it will be your time.

As for my life, I am kind of like the tomato plant that everyone thought was dead; maybe your story is similar. I have surpassed and flourished beyond belief because it is all God's timing and not ours. I have seen, over my years, some of the most intelligent, successful, and powerful people simply lose their minds. I truly believe when God says he will make your enemies a thing of naught, he means it.

One particular person comes to mind; in the prime of his career, he was a strong and powerful person. Every day, he commanded large groups of men and women. When he talked, people listened. This man was successful, handsome, and terrifying. When it came to this man, it was not about doing things the right way; it was about doing it his way. If you crossed him, regardless if you did the correct thing, his punishment was swift and cruel. If you stood by a person on the side of right, this man would punish you severely. This man enjoyed making anyone who opposed him miserable. I was one of those people; he (unjustly) hated me. This man was mean, and because of his power and success, he was arrogant and full of pride.

However, after a long time being held in this sucky position, I came into work one day and he was gone. He retired suddenly; nobody spoke about it or knew why. He was simply gone. A few years ago, I heard after this person completed a conversation with a family member, this person excused himself and then walked into the basement and killed himself. Life happens.

As time passes, none of us will remain the prettiest, the smartest, or strongest. So it is a must to have the fullness of joy that only comes from an intimate relationship with Jesus. Not all plants that grow the fastest remain the greatest in the long run. Keep your head down and move in the flow of the Holy Spirit. Remember, God says your future will be greater than your past.

"And though you started with little, you will end with much." –Job 8:7

CHAPTER 15:

FLY LIKE AN EAGLE

My strength comes every morning when, through the Holy Spirit, I put on my full armor of God. I have found this renewing must be done daily, and it only occurs in worship and prayer sessions. It's basically pressing into God and requesting some personal time with him. God truly requires our love and relationship with him to be personal and intimate. I used to turn on the TV and have my coffee while I watched the early news, but then the Lord pressed upon my heart he would like to spend time with me first. How awesome is it that our God of the universe wants to speak with us, spend time with us? I don't know about you, but with me, a cup of coffee has always signified a time of fellowship with family, friends, or co-workers. Yes, it's true; most cops do like doughnuts with their coffee; it's a perfect combo.

I think God uses different things with different people; your thing might be tea. God will speak to you in the love language you know. For me, I only have coffee with people I want to be around, so it is with God. What I do is get my coffee and sit down in my living room (my war room) to be quiet with God. I do this every day before my prayer and worship sessions. This simple shift has made such a tremendous shift in my prayer life and in my life period. I challenge you to try it and see what happens. God has to be the first in everything you do every day. Rain or sun, in sickness or in health, blessings or disasters, God *must* be the first thing you do every day.

So Isaiah and Ephesians go hand in hand to me. You approach the throne of God every morning with praise and worship (I like music); that accomplishes it for me and brings me into the presence of God. Once in God's presence, begin to put on the full armor of God. Speak out into the atmosphere who God is and what he has done for you. Speak into the atmosphere what mountains God has he moved for you and trust him to move all future mountains. This is your best position of faith. This is letting hell know it does not matter what it looks like now, but my God—my Jesus can do it for me. Think about it: failure is not an option for God. Victory is what he is and what he does. Go team Jesus.

As you repent of any sin and come into agreement with God's will for your life, you are righteous. Our Father

God sees us in right standing with him. Why? Because of his Son, Jesus Christ, and the blood he shed for you on Calvary. You put on your belt of truth, which is Jesus and your helmet of Salvation, because nothing separates you from the love and saving grace of Jesus. Know who you are in Christ. You are forgiven, you are delivered, and you are healed.

As you speak out the Word of God and discuss all the issues, yes even your issues you keep hidden deep in your heart, God is listening. You now have face time with God. Also, it's a good idea to write down and learn a few Scriptures. Usually God gives you a few that are

"Use every piece of God's armor to resist the enemy in the time of evil, so that after the battle you will still be standing firm. Stand your ground, putting on the sturdy belt of truth and the body armor of God's righteousness. For shoes, put on the peace that comes from the Good News, so that you will be fully prepared. In every battle you will need faith as your shield to stop the fiery arrows aimed at you by Satan. Put on salvation as your helmet, and take the sword of the Spirit, which is the word of God. Pray at all times and on every occasion in the power of the Holy Spirit. Stay alert and be persistent in your prayers for all Christians everywhere." –Ephesians 6:13-18

meant for you. I love "And we know that all things work together for good to them that love God, to them who are the called according to his purpose." Romans 8:28. Find your Scriptures and speak them into the atmosphere (watch what happens). You have now utilized your only offensive weapon; provided in your suit of armor: *your sword*, which is the Word of God.

At the end of your audience with the King of kings, you will be renewed and revitalized.

What type of bird are you? Have you ever watched an eagle fly? They soar; they do not flap their wings around in vain as the smaller birds do. They go twice as far with one pump of their mighty wings than a smaller bird travels with numerous flaps of their wings. They expend less energy and get further than the smaller birds do. I know that is what happens to people whom make a practice of placing God first, they soar.

As with any habit, good or bad, the more you do it, the better (if it's good) or the worse (if it's bad) you become. I promise you, if you make it a habit of allowing the Holy Spirit to renew, heal, and deliver you (continually) your heavy burdens are replaced by wings to fly. Your wings will allow you to glide upon life's everchanging winds. If you have a minute to watch a big bird fly, you will notice the larger birds use a lot less effort to stay in the air. The smaller birds make me tired watching them. I know scientists can explain why there is such a different wingspan and air flow, but I know what the Lord told my heart one day as I watched the falcons fly around over my backyard.

I was on my back deck in the month of March so there were not many leaves on the trees. The trees are just beginning to bud at this time. So you get a mental picture, I live on a huge mountain, and there are woods behind my yard as well as other neighbors' homes. For various reasons, the falcons choose to fly, hunt, and perch on the tall high school football stadium light poles, located in the rear of my house. Even though these creatures were perched on the stadium poles, far off distance I could easily see (even with my bad eyes) these were large birds.

Now, I have lived in this location for twenty years but have never noticed this many falcons in the past. Lately, for some reason, the falcons are coming close to my house and yard, I guessed, maybe to hunt. My back deck gives me a front row seat, and it's a fascinating thing to watch.

Usually when God is showing me something he wants me to remember, time slows down; sort of like slow motion on TV or a movie.

I have learned over time to be still and listen; it's God's way of saying, "Watch this." I used to try to understand this but now, I am privileged God shows me his presence in ordinary everyday things. God is always speaking to us, but we are not always listening.

As I stood on my deck enjoying one of the first semi-warm days since winter broke, I looked up to give God thanks for keeping my family and me and noticed three or four huge falcons flying around my backyard and surrounding area. These falcons were so close; my first instinct was to take off running over to my neighbor's house to warn them to get their small black dog in the house. Their dog is the size of my hand and would be easy pickings for these large birds. It appeared as if these falcons were on the hunt because they were organized and appeared to have a mission. My husband told me one day, he was outside and he saw, from a distance, one of the falcons dive into the woods and rise again with what looked to be a snake in its claws.

The falcons were so close; it was a magnificent sight, and my heart beat from part excitement and maybe a little fear because of their closeness. It was an early Saturday morning and nobody was out yet, so I wanted to yell out, "Is anybody else seeing this?" I am certain this is not a sight you see every day. As the Lord calmed my heart, he said, "Watch," and I noticed how these beautiful birds flew. They did not dive at anything; they weaved in and out of each other, glided and rarely flapped their wings. The falcons glided on the wind, never afraid the wind would stop causing them to plummet to the ground. The falcons flew confidently, majestically. I was in awe. God whispered to my soul, "This is how it is when you *trust me*. You will glide in and out of the seasons of your life on the power of my Holy Spirit." God said again, "Trust me." We must trust God's Holy Spirit to uphold us, as the falcons trusted the wind to uphold them.

As I heard this in my soul, I looked to the left and saw other smaller birds fluttering from rooftop to rooftop using what looked to me to be a lot of energy. These smaller birds never reached the heights of the falcons, and they appeared to be content. I made up my mind then, and maybe before this moment, I am and will never be content with fluttering house to house like the smaller birds. God promised abundant life, so I am going to jump and let the Holy Spirit be the wind beneath my wings.

God wants all of us to be falcons, but many Christians are content with flying around in their daily lives like the little birds are content with going to church every day; never tapping into the greatest resource called Jesus Christ, God. The question is again, are you a falcon or little bird?

As a Christian, you belong to God. Jesus has bought and paid for you soul totally; so you have all the perks that come along with the wonderful gift of Salvation. Being reconciled to the Father through Christ is *your inheritance.* However, God must have first place in everything. The enemy will do everything possible to get you to move God into second and third place.

One of Satan's favorite tools is distraction; whether it is a good or bad distraction does not matter. For me, a good distraction would be extra clients for my polygraph business. Success is good, but it can also be a tool Satan uses against you, if you're not careful. I have found whatever it might be, if it shifts God out of first place in your life, it's a problem. You must realign your life, which can be difficult when it's fun stuff like spending time with my grandson. So yes, nothing, not even family responsibility, comes before your time and relationship with God.

I find when I keep God first in my life, he allows me to utilize the rest of my time in a more productive way. I find I am ultra-effective professionally and enjoy my family and leisure time more intensely. I know, realistically we have the same numbers of hours in a day, but I am able to accomplish so much more in one day. I rest in the ability of God and all of this would be outrageously impossible without him.

I am fifty-two years old, and my plate is full with an unbelievably stressful full-time job, growing business, and husband, daughter, and grandson. I wake up at four a.m. on most days and don't stop until bedtime at eleven p.m. When God says, **"You shall run and not grow weary"**

He means it.

"But those who wait on the Lord will find new strength. They will fly high on wings like eagles. They will run and not grow weary. They will walk and not faint." –Isaiah 40:31

Over the years of my sometimes-painful life, I have somehow, through the grace of God, grown wings. I have wings, and it is truly wonderful. Once you get a taste of realization that God can truly do *all things*, you will never ever settle for flying from rooftop to rooftop again. The only way you will travel is by soaring on the tailwinds of God's Holy Spirit. God did say his yoke is easier, and after observing the difference in the way a big bird flies, I choose God's yoke. I hope you do also.

"For my yoke fits perfectly, and the burden I give you is light." –Matthew 11:30

CHAPTER 16:

THIS MEANS WAR!

*M*aybe you are the Christian who strives to be a servant of God; do you strain to hear the voice of God? Do you call on God to fight your battles and protect your family? Good, maintain your position. This world is a dark place that seeks to steal any light and joy that you gain. Yet every morning, you manage to seek one moment in time, to crawl into the presence of our Lord Jesus Christ. You strain to touch the hem of his garment because in the touch, you are healed; in the touch, you are revitalized to battle one more day. Trust your actions are not in vain; trust in the Lord with all your heart, mind, body, and soul, because when you least expect it, your prayers will be answered. When it is your season, there will be nothing that can come against you.

Listen. People of God, your season is now. Your secret weapon in this season will be worship. This season is like no other season for us Christians. Worship is an aggressive attack against hell and all its demons. Worship is your battle cry because, whether you know it or not, we are at war. If you are a true person of God, life is been rather hard lately. You might be feeling oppressed and overwhelmed in even the simplest of areas. This is not your imagination; this is Satan throwing his last "Hail Mary" pass. Again, I say, maintain your position! The Lord has put on my heart worship is the way; we are victorious now. It has never been more important to put God first by glorifying his holy name. God's praise must go out and up before God moves on our behalf. God's people can no longer fight in their own strength. It was never a good idea, but NOW, if you take the time to praise before you petition God, I promise you will see a supernatural move in your life.

I talked to one of my co-workers, and he said he talked to God about his wife being sick, and he told God, "Dude, do you really f—-ing want to put me in charge of things? Not a good idea." He continued to tell me, he and God know each other and they both have a sense of humor. True, I believe our God has a wonderful sense of humor. He created all of us, and he gave laughter to us as a gift, but please don't get it twisted. God is God, and he is Holy. You do not approach the mighty throne of God, in any kind of way. Let me be clear: *God is not one of us.*

"The Lord is King! Let the nations tremble! He sits on his throne between the cherubim. Let the whole earth quake! The Lord sits in majesty in Jerusalem, supreme above all nations. Let them praise your great and awesome name. Your Name is holy!" –Psalm 99:1-3

"Exalt the Lord our God! Bow low before his feet, for he is holy!" –Psalm 99:5

The word "holy" means set apart from that which is unclean and that which is common. So it is not only unclean stuff, but God is set apart from the ordinary. We serve a God who knows he is God, but this world (including Christians) tends to make God common. God is not ordinary; he is Holy and we should treat him with the honor he deserves.

Note: when we stand to read the Holy Word of God, we are giving God honor. Because of Jesus, we have access to our Holy Father.

In the Old Testament, the name of God was written, because the name of God was too holy to speak verbally. The Scribes had to stop writing and go take a full bath before they could go onto write the name of our Holy God. Can you imagine if one sentence called for God's name to be written several times? That's a lot of baths. Now we, because of Jesus, are not under the old law, but again it is a heart matter we must respect God's holiness. As I said before, God will not accept anything less than first place. So how do we get into the correct position? To me, the perfect instructional manual is 2 Chronicles 20. It's a step by step instruction on how you get into the correct position to receive God's words and favor. The King of Judah at the time was Jehoshaphat, and he got word the vast army of Edom was against him and his people. Not that they wanted to do this—*no*, they were already headed his way. Now Judah had an army, but they did not compare to the force coming against them. Sort of like the USA declaring war and marching against a small country; they may have an army, but it's no match against us.

"Jehoshaphat stood before the people of Judah and Jerusalem in front of the new courtyard at the Temple of the Lord. He prayed, 'O Lord, God of our ancestors, you alone are the God who is in heaven. You are ruler of all the kingdoms of the earth. You are powerful and mighty; no one can stand against you!'" –2 Chronicles 20:5-6

What the king and his people did first was place God first by giving him his *glory*. Going to God should be the first thing we do when problems arise, not when all else fails. God is not ever plan B; he's plan A, B, and C. God, in this season, demands to be plan A. Have you ever heard someone say, "God is my co-pilot"? I believe God is my pilot. Not only did he make the co-pilot (*you*), but he made the plane and the atmosphere and everything else.

In 2 Chronicles 20:9, the king goes one step further to petition a move of God. The king and the people declared their faith in God's ability.

"They said, 'Whenever we are faced with any calamity such as war, disease, or famine, we can come to stand in your presence before this Temple where your name is honored. We can cry out to you to save us, and you will hear us and rescue us.'" —2 Chronicles 20:9

The king and his people declare they had faith in God's ability. They basically are saying, "God, you are our protector, provider, deliverer, and healer." These are some of the names of God.

"As all the men of Judah stood before the Lord with their little ones, wives, and children, the Spirit of the Lord came upon one of the men standing there. His name was Jahaziel son of Zechariah, son of Benaiah, son of Jeiel, son of Mattaniah, a Levite who was a descendant of Asaph."
—2 Chronicles 20:13-14

The Spirit of the Lord came upon the man ***after*** the king and his people had properly positioned themselves to receive the outpouring of God's favor.

"He said, 'Listen King Jehoshaphat! Listen all you people of Judah and Jerusalem! This is what the Lord says: Do not be afraid! Don't be discouraged by this mighty army, for the battle is not yours, but God's.'" –2 Chronicles 20:15-18

Every time I read this, I think how many battles had I fought that were not even mine to fight.

"Tomorrow, march out against them. You will find them coming up through the ascent of Ziz at the end of the valley that opens into the wilderness of Jeruel." –2 Chronicles 20:16

God is in the details—not the devil, God! He inhabits the praise of his people, us.

"But you will not even need to fight. Take your positions; then stand still and watch the LORD's victory. He is with you, O people of Judah and Jerusalem. Do not be afraid or discouraged. Go out tomorrow, for the LORD is with you!"
—2 Chronicles 20:17 (NLT)

Now let me explain what "take your position" means (we use it often in police settings). It means be on the ready. Come dressed for battle. There is nothing worse than God calling you to take your position, and you show up wearing flip-flops and pajama pants.

"Then King Jehoshaphat bowed down with his face to the ground. And all the people of Judah and Jerusalem did the same, worshiping the Lord."
—2 Chronicles 20:18

Understand faith is God's Word, believed!_The people gave God glory and thanked God (worshiped

God) before they saw anything physically in this fleshly realm. Our faith activates God's power.

"Early the next morning the army of Judah went out into the Wilderness of Tekoa. On the way Jehoshaphat stopped and said, 'Listen to me, all you people of Judah and Jerusalem! Believe in the Lord your God, and you will be able to stand firm. Believe in his prophets, and you will succeed."
—2 Chronicles 20:20

In verses 21 and 22, after consulting with his leaders of the people, the king appointed singers to *walk ahead of the army,* singing to the Lord and praising him for his holy splendor.

They sang, **"Give thanks to the Lord; his faithful love endures *forever!*"**

To give you a mental picture of this, a few years ago, the city of Pittsburgh hosted the G-20 International. It was a huge ordeal; we were specially trained and received special equipment. All the police officers (including me) were on the television wearing riot helmets, full armor vests, shields guns, Tasers, nightsticks, and pepper spray. Got the picture? Okay, now picture before we moved out onto the front lines, the command staff ordered the unarmed church choir or worship team to go out in front of the fully armed police force. God does the impossible. Praise and worship is how we will have victory in this season.

"At the moment they began to sing and give praise, the Lord caused the armies of Ammon, Moab, and Mount Seir to start fighting among themselves."
–2 Chronicles 20:22

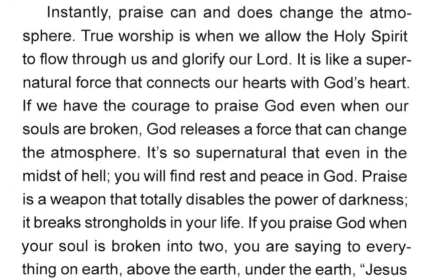

Instantly, praise can and does change the atmosphere. True worship is when we allow the Holy Spirit to flow through us and glorify our Lord. It is like a supernatural force that connects our hearts with God's heart. If we have the courage to praise God even when our souls are broken, God releases a force that can change the atmosphere. It's so supernatural that even in the midst of hell; you will find rest and peace in God. Praise is a weapon that totally disables the power of darkness; it breaks strongholds in your life. If you praise God when your soul is broken into two, you are saying to everything on earth, above the earth, under the earth, "Jesus Christ is Lord and he will keep me." In this season, we must activate this weapon called praise.

Praise is not dependent on how you feel or your circumstance. It is dependent on who God is and his awesome ability. All is possible with God. Man-no. God-yes.

To continue on the subject of worship, I want to speak about tithes and offerings. Yes, I know what some are saying. How the heck are they related? Well, as we praise God because of who he is, we trust God is fully capable of keeping us in every situation. When we tithe, we are telling God the same exact thing. We are saying, "I trust you." If we, as humans, like to hear someone tell us they trust us, imagine the blessings that come from God, when we demonstrate with our actions that we trust him. Stepping out in faith activates God's blessings.

I do not say these things haphazardly, or say them because Christians are told by the church they should tithe. No, I say this because the Word of God tells us we should trust him enough to know he will provide for us. Also, I have put God to the test. By the way, this is the only area God gives us permission to test him. It's not a great idea to go around blatantly testing the Almighty God of the universe. Here is what God says about his people breaking covenant by withholding tithes:

"I am the Lord, and I do not change. That is why you descendants of Jacob are not already completely destroyed. Ever since the days of your ancestors, you have scorned my laws and failed to obey them. Now return to me, and I will return to you," says the Lord Almighty. "But you ask, 'How can we return when we have never gone away?' "Should people cheat God? Yet you have cheated me! "But you ask, 'What do you mean? When did we ever cheat you?' "You have cheated me of the tithes and offerings due to me. You are under a curse, for your whole nation has been cheating me. Bring all the tithes into the storehouse so there will be enough food in my Temple. If you do," says the Lord Almighty, "I will open the windows of heaven to you. I will pour out a blessing so great you won't have enough room to take it in! Try it! Let me prove it to you! Your crops will be abundant, for I will guard them from insects and disease. Your grapes will not shrivel before they are ripe," says the Lord Almighty. 'Then all nations will call you blessed, for your land will be such a delight,' says the Lord Almighty.'" –Malachi 3:6-12

Tithing works because it's a promise from him to you, but you still must step out in faith and trust him at his word. Let us dive into what God is saying here. In the beginning, God says his people are robbing him.

He says this because everything we have belongs to him. So when you get your paycheck, your tithes should come off your gross income before taxes are taken out.

Jesus said in the New Testament he did not come to change Scriptures, but he came to fulfill them. So the requirements of tithing did not change when Jesus entered the world. In Matthew 22:21 (after he showed them a coin), Jesus asked whose picture was on the coin, and the people replied, "Caesar." Jesus then said to them, "So give back to Caesar what is Caesar's, and to God what is God's." Caesar represents the government. When you pay your taxes, you are giving Caesar his cut. There no choice in giving Caesar his money, but the decision to tithe is all your choice. God will not force you in this matter, because tithes are a heart issue.

When God says the nation is under a curse, I feel poverty can be a generational stronghold and a curse. If our parents don't understand the principles of tithing or good financial habits, it's rare that the child will develop in this area. The first thing you need to do if you are financially challenged is tithe; yes, give money. This will release the curse from you, your household, and your generations. God does say bring your tithes and offering into the storehouse so there would be food in his house. We must, as Christians, find and keep a church home so this principle will operate properly. Our churches are closing because we, as a people, are not attending church regularly, and then when we do attend, we refuse to tithe.

One of my favorite scriptures to read is Malachi. God basically says if you doubt him on tithes and offering, then test him on this matter. No, it doesn't mean money instantly falls from the sky. What I have found is my God is faithful and blessings happen. The Lord says to test him on this because he knows we are human and this is a strange concept for us to grasp. Tithing goes against human logic. Any financial (worldly) expert will tell you tithing is a waste of your money. Do not put God in our humanly defined box.

I also say until you get used to tithing principles, don't think too hard and long on that check you're writing because your human logic will kick in. Just as Peter stepped out in faith when he got out the boat to walk on the water to get to Jesus, we have to step out in faith with tithes. Remember, as long as Peter kept his eyes on God, he was fine. As soon as Peter said to himself, "Wait, I am walking on water," (human logic) he began to sink. However, our Lord instantly put out his hand and saved him. Get out of the boat, write the check, and move on.

Now God goes one better. He says not only will he bless you beyond your wildest imaginations, but he will *prevent* the canker worm or pest from devouring your crops. Your crops in this day and age are your paycheck, your money, and your goods. A good example of a pest or cankerworm is an identity thief. To me, this promise from God is better than the Life Lock Company. Still, be mindful about how you conduct your financial business, but truly our Almighty Lord has got our backs.

God also says he will not allow your vines to drop fruit before their time. Timing is everything with money and business as it is in most things. If a crop of fruit ripens at the wrong time, it is costly to the farmer. I have seen God bless me so many times in my business matters; it amazes me. God's perfect timing will always produce amazing results.

In the last verse, God says other nations will call your land "blessed." I feel, at least in my life, God will not bless you in the dark, but he will bless you openly for all to see. People will see and remark how blessed you are; you will live in your overflow and be a blessing to all those around you. You will become the head and not the tail; you become the lender, not the borrower.

Please remember God did not create tithes for his benefit; God created tithing and offerings for our benefit. God clearly says in his word if you are obedient with your tithes and offerings, he will bless you to the point you can't contain it. Tithes and offerings give God a spiritually legal way to bless you. Why? Because God cannot lie. He must honor his own word.

CONCLUSION:

THE TRIP OF A LIFETIME

*T*his is the time of our human existence to walk by faith and trust the Lord. Everybody says, "God bless you," or, "I trust in the Lord." It has become a phrase as common as saying "God bless you" when somebody sneezes.

I thought I trusted God, but one time in early 2014, God showed me through an experience that I had not yet totally given myself over to him. I did trust God, but not the kind of trust God required of me in the upcoming season of my life.

Before I tell you this story, I had to first muster up the courage to tell my husband about this experience. I was a bit nervous because I did want him to start making plans to have me committed. After I sheepishly told him what I will tell you, to my astonishment, he said he totally listened and truly believed what I told him. He actually appeared to be living it with me as I talked.

Let me explain a little about my husband's character. He is not the type of man who will agree with me if I am off base on an issue. He is the type of man who is straightforward; he does not smile if he doesn't feel like smiling. I have learned over my fourteen-year marriage to him, it is not a good idea to ask his opinion about something if I didn't want a brutally truthful answer. Over the years, however, I feel he has learned to deflect certain questions like if I looked fat in or out of my outfit.

Anyway, after telling my husband about my experience, I decided to tell my Faith Keepers group. Faith Keepers is a group of ladies who meet every second Wednesday of every month to fellowship. We eat, pray, and talk about our favorite subject: Jesus Christ. We are a racially diverse group of women who range from thirty-five to seventy-five years of age. I trust each one of the women in this group. I value their honest opinions on the many issues we discuss regarding family, children, and life.

I don't know how it came up, but somehow during one of these meetings, I decided to open my mouth and tell the ladies about my experience. Again, to my surprise, they listened intently to me repeat this experience. Each lady added her piece of Godly wisdom about my experience. This is why, as Christians, we

need to fellowship with other believers. If left to ourselves, we will tend to live by our own truth. You need
to filter your thoughts through God, and his word and
godly trusted people he puts in your life.

Well, at the end of my story, one of the women, out
of the blue, said, "You should put that in your book." I
believe this was from God, and confirmation of what
I had wrestled with in my mind. It was a year earlier I
shared with the women of my Faith Keepers group; I
felt the Lord pressing on my heart to write a book. So
I decided to be totally transparent and put this experience in this book.

This event occurred in 2014. If it had occurred around
my brother's untimely death, I would have thought this
experience was related to that terribly stressful incident.
No, this event occurred one mid-spring chilly morning

It was a typical day for me. I had to get up earlier than usual to pray, get dressed, and do my normal
criminal court walk. After you arrest a person, the case
eventually will get to the last phase of the legal process, which is the criminal prosecution. The defendant
will either accept a plea or go to trial. There is often a
postponement or a continuation on the day the trial is
set to go. Criminal Court cases can be postponed upon
the request of the defendant's attorney or the assistant
district attorney assigned to prosecute the case.

For the police officer, we are required to check into the courthouse by 8:30 a.m. whether the case is going forward or not. It was decided by the assistant district attorney assigned to this case it would be postponed to another date. So I was able to leave the courthouse, after a few hours of being there.

On this day, I did not have to be in my office until later, so I decided to go home to eat and rest before going into my office. Once home, I took off my suit and hung it on the banister because I planned to wear the same suit to the office later. I put on my favorite plush snuggly white robe that my mom gave me for Christmas. This robe was more like a grey robe now because it had been washed and worn so many times.

I made a light lunch and sat on the couch in the living room to eat it. The house was quiet because my husband was still asleep upstairs in our bedroom. At this time, he worked a six p.m. to two a.m. shift as the Impact Narcotics Sergeant. By the time he got home and in bed, it was four a.m., so he did not wake up until noon or one p.m. the next day.

I felt good; nothing in particular bothered me. I decided to watch one of my "Diagnosis: Murder" recorded episodes starring Dick Van Dyke and his son as the lead detective. I love this show and Colombo, and I record every episode.

As I lay down on the couch in my favorite position to watch television, I laid on my left side, in a semi-fetal position. The next thing I knew, I was aware of my self-sleeping on the couch. The weird part here is I was aware of me on the couch because I hovered about three or four feet over me. Yep, you heard it right; I hovered three to four feet above my head. My head rested on the pillow I had put on the armrest of the couch. I was fully aware I wasn't awake yet because I could still see my body asleep on the couch. I could see the closet door behind me, and I hovered toward the top of this closet door. I was above the lamp and wine rack located directly behind my head. About the same time I started to realize this was like no other dream I had ever had. I also began to notice I could see the objects and myself on the couch without turning my head. I could see 360-degrees around the room at the same time. My mind actually processed information just as I am doing now.

Strangely, I was not afraid. As I thought to myself, *this is a dream*, I instantly gained knowledge from a non-verbal independent source (other than me) this was not a dream. I looked closer at myself lying on the couch. I know it sounds totally loopy. I remember seeing my hair as it lay on the couch pillow; I recall every crease of my dingy white robe.

Almost instantly, I knew I was in a different place, a place where the air was still or non-existent. I also knew

I was not alone despite I could only see my body lying on the couch in the living room. Another strange thing is I could see, but I did not have eyes or a body. As I looked at the different objects in the room, there was no part of my body blocking the view. The only way I can describe this to you is if you stop reading and look down to the floor. You should see your legs or your feet as you look at the floor. I saw the floor, but there was no body.

I then thought to myself, *I must be dead.* I tried to look at my body to see if I was breathing, but I was prevented from getting any closer than three to four feet. In the same moment, I pondered that I might be dead, and understanding came to my mind that it did not matter whether I was alive or dead. God was with me. When I call this voice "understanding," that is what it was. When the voice spoke to my mind, which was not audible, I had instant understanding.

All I can explain is every bit of faith I lived my life with was now with me as I hovered over my body. I was not cold; I was not sad; I was not alone.

In this instant, I had understanding. I now understood because Jesus Christ owned Ethan's soul, he was claimed and his soul was spoken for already. The portion of God that was placed in Ethan—the Holy Spirit (no matter how underdeveloped it was)—was with him always. Remember, nothing can separate you from Christ.

This issue in my heart was finally put to rest, and it is well with my soul. At that moment, I said, "I trust you Lord," and I instantly began to float/move up to the celling and surprisingly through my floor to the bedroom where Nate slept. I went through the floor with no problem; it was like walking from one room into another room.

I saw my husband in our bed still asleep; he had the pillow on his head. He has a habit of doing this some-times when he is in a deep sleep. I did not see the TV on, but the room was still dark from the blinds being closed. The house was still, as it would have been if I had walked through it. I continued to drift upward, I still did not see anybody or anything with me but yet, I was totally aware I was not alone. I went through the floor again, into the attic, which was now a spare bedroom, since Ethan had died.

I drifted through the roof, which was totally strange, because now I floated above my house. I wish I had thought to check the condition of my roof while I was up there. I fear it will need replacing soon. Anyway, I could see the tops of my neighbors' houses. I was outside, but I was not cold. I don't recall feeling a breeze as I moved through the air. I floated, a little like flying but I did not have wings. I or we (because I was not alone) took me down a little ways from the rooftops to about the level of my second floor window. We began to move down the street away from my home, and I could see inside the neighbor's second floor windows.

I remember looking into the windows because I wanted to see if anybody could see me. The weird thing is, I could see through the windows and into the houses themselves, but did not see any of my neighbors. At this time of day, they would have been at work, but as I looked into the windows, I saw many people that appeared small and transparent, but visible enough to see. They were not children, but these beings were different from me. They were void of light or life. There were about fifty or more of these beings standing in one room looking out the window. Their faces were void of expression as they looked at me float past. I got the impression these beings saw me.

I literally floated down my street and made a left. I floated, but I became aware I was still curled up in the same fetal position; my body laid before all this began. This was weird because I had no physical body. I said again, "Lord, I trust you," and I felt a release. It felt as if my soul stretched out. I felt huge and wonderful. Now, I no longer floated, I flew.

When I stretched out and embraced what was going on, I felt free, totally whole. This was liberating; I was complete. I was not afraid, even though I am not crazy about heights. I now flew. It felt like the being that helped me fly was a part of my core being. I did not have wings, but I had the understanding I was not alone and I did not fly on my own.

I recall seeing my entire neighborhood as if I para-sailed down my streets. We then began to fly through Pittsburgh. I recall seeing many of our bridges and land-marks around town through an aerial view. We moved faster, and I remember getting a little higher, and then higher. I could no longer make out any of the objects on the ground. I have traveled in airplanes, so I've seen this before from this view. I still was not afraid.

We then began to move faster, and faster. I felt no wind, but assumed we moved faster because the objects on the ground were smaller and smaller as we quickly passed them. I recall as our pace quickened, I had the realization we were also going higher and higher into a place I had never seen before. I recalled going through what looked to be clouds and then past the clouds and then what looked to be dim or darker skies, all along communicating with what I believe to be my Holy Spirit. The job of the Holy Spirit, Jesus said, was to guide, exhort, and edify us. The Holy Spirit is with us always, once we have accepted Christ as our Lord and Savior. He never fails nor forsakes us, and he leads us to God's truth. I believe the Holy Spirit's job does not stop when we leave our fleshly bodies; he is with us always, which means past death and into eternity.

"And I will ask the Father, and he will give you another Counselor, who will never leave you. He is the Holy Spirit, who leads into all truth. The world at large cannot receive him, because it isn't looking for him and doesn't recognize him. But you do, because he lives with you now and later will be in you." –John 14:16-17

During this entire experience, I was in constant communication with something, but no words were necessary. We communicated nonverbally and non-visually, but the understanding between us was clear and precise. I think words are something God gave us as humans to communicate with each other and him here on earth.

My Holy Spirit was with me inside me, but it was distinctly separate from me as we moved along this journey. As we traveled up and up, I realized we left earth. The skies around me became dark, and I remember thinking it looked cold and icy, but I was not cold. I remember seeing the earth as we moved far above the clouds. I could see what looked to be large bodies of water and land, but by no means could I make out anything else on the ground.

Then I realized I left our atmosphere. What was ahead of me was truly nothing like I had ever seen. Pictures of outer space don't do it justice. It was totally exciting and downright scary all at the same time. Never in my life did I have any, and I mean any, desire to go into space. I had understanding; soon the earth would be behind me. Now I was afraid.

I left what I had known for fifty-one years. I wondered would God bring me back? Was I going to be with God, which meant I would be dead? I was confused suddenly. I began to wonder how would it look if my husband got up and found me dead on the couch. I was worried about my daughter and grandson and what would happen without me there. It was strange, but I knew still I was not alone, but I didn't hear anything from my Holy Spirit (the voice) anymore. It was like we had stopped moving upward and in that instant, in a flash of a moment, I traveled down, fast.

We moved at the speed of light, or so it felt. We had to be moving fast because I could not make out any landmarks as I had done before. As I descended through the atmosphere, I begin to feel heavy or burdened again. I felt the lower I got, I put on another layer of clothing. As I traveled downward through a particular group of clouds, it was like my sexual desire was activated. Then I went through something sexually perverse. All I know, when I came out the other end, it felt

179

like I had just viewed many hours of raunchy, hard core porn movies.

We live in a dark, prevised, and crooked world. Perhaps this is the atmosphere I returned to. Before my thoughts could catch up, I was back at my house and traveled quickly back into my body. I entered my body again with the sound of a pop. I felt like I was a huge balloon being stuffed into a little tiny box. With the sound of the pop, I sat straight up and was fully awake, on the couch.

I knew instantly something had happened that was different from any dream I had ever had. First, it is rare I remember my dreams, and second, I felt as though I had physically gotten back from an errand or something. I tried to wrap my mind around what had happened. I wanted to run upstairs and wake up my husband, but I thought he would feel like I was crazy.

I started to think again this was a dream, but as I looked at the TV show I had turned on before my trip began, I noticed I had not missed anything. I watch the same reruns of this show over and over again, so I knew no time had passed. If this were a dream, the television program I had on would have been further along in the show. Time had not passed in the usual manner.

I decided to ask God what all this meant. I thought it would be one of those issues I would have to fast and petition God for an answer. Nope, before I could barely get out the question, God said, "You didn't trust me enough to take you into the atmosphere." I wonder what could have happened if I didn't lose faith and get scared? Did I miss a wonderful blessing? I know God seeks only the best for me, so I continually strive to grow to where God wants me to be. Right when you think you got it together, I find God wants you to take it a step higher. Fruit to more fruit.

I believe God is making a final call to the thirsty, the people he has called and designated according to his purpose. We are the thirsty, the servants of our Lord Jesus Christ. God has anointed you!

"Is anyone thirsty? Come and drink—even if you have no money! Come, take your choice of wine or milk—it's all free! Why spend your money on food that does not give you strength? Why pay for food that does you no good? Listen, and I will tell you where to get food that is good for the soul! Come to me with your ears wide open. Listen, for the life of your soul is at stake. I am ready to make an everlasting covenant with you. I will give you all the mercies and unfailing love that I promised to David." –Isaiah 55:1-3

When I read the above scriptures, it is clear God seeks a personal relationship with his people. We only talk this way to people we deeply love and care about greatly.

The living water is our Lord Jesus Christ, and the everlasting covenant, God says he will make with us, is the **free gift of salvation**. Because of Jesus, we have the same faithful love he promised to King David. This kind of love affair with God requires (if you're brave enough) to totally *trust* God to take you into the atmosphere!

It is done.

**Left to Right, unknown police
officer and my Dad - Earl Buford Sr.**

**Left to Right- My Dad and
brother Ethan.**

The Dough Boy

My home at 16 years old.

Ethan Moore: 4/8/1967 to 7/29/2013…"you I loved."

ACKNOWLEDGMENTS

I would like to once again thank my Holy Father God for all he has provided me in the way of love and support from my family.

The word of God says, "He who finds a wife finds a good thing." Well, I believe she who finds a good husband has found a good thing as well. My husband loves me and even more importantly, he loves God more than me. Now that's a sweet package.

I am thankful for my adult daughter. She has been with me for twenty-six years and her love is tried, true, and steadfast. Since she was a little girl, she would tell me again and again, "Mom, when you get old, I will take care of you. I will wipe your bottom, just like you did when I was a baby." I don't know how you feel about that, but to me, that's love, big time. I am blessed to look into the eyes of my grandson. God does take away, but he adds so much more.

I have been blessed with a mother and a sister who have always believed I could do anything, even when I failed miserably at it.

I thank God for good friends who stand by me even when it's raining. Pastor Donna McKinley, who mentored me from my comfortable seat on our church pew, to the uncomfortable position of presiding. I thank Dr. Elder Renee Galloway for her willingness to share her knowledge she gained while writing her own book. I am especially grateful for the leadership of my pastors, Neville and Connie Brooks. I thank and love all the women in my Faith Keepers group. Each one of you encouraged me to reach for my dreams while resting firmly in Jesus Christ. Paul and Rose, you are my friends, and yes, AKA family forever. I thank God for the simple things because the greatest gifts and blessings are the simplest ones.

Special Thanks to: Mrs. June King, Retired Pittsburgh Police Assistant Chief, Maurita Bryant and Rewind Media LLC.

ABOUT THE AUTHOR

Tamara Hawthorne

Tamara Hawthorne was born in Pittsburgh, Pennsylvania to Earl Buford Sr. and Nancy Moore. Tamara Hawthorne has been a Pittsburgh police officer for twenty-seven years. The first five years of her law enforcement career involved duties such as patrol officer, uniformed drug task force officer, and training academy instructor. In 1994, Tamara Hawthorne had the opportunity to become a Pittsburgh Police Detective in the Sex Assault and Child Abuse Unit. Over the last twenty-four years, Detective Hawthorne has investigated and helped criminally prosecute over eight hundred child abuse cases. Currently, Tamara Hawthorne is the senior detective who oversees the Pittsburgh Police Department's newly formed Domestic Violence Unit.

In 2011, Detective Hawthorne became the first black female polygraph examiner for the Pittsburgh Police Department. Upon graduating from the Virginia School of Polygraph, Tamara Hawthorne received (along with her diploma) the Director's Merit Award for Outstanding Academics. In 2012, Tamara Hawthorne continued her polygraph education and was certified as a Post-Conviction Sex Offender Examiner by the Virginia School of Polygraph.

In 2014, God blessed Tamara with the opportunity to open her own polygraph private practice, located at:
445 Fort Pitt Blvd.
Pittsburgh, PA 15219
GG Polygraph and Interview Services is another example of God making the impossible possible.

ABOUT THE AUTHOR
CONTINUED

*T*amara is involved in many women and children outreach and community projects/programs through her affiliations with the National Organizations of Black Law Enforcement Executives, the Pittsburgh Police Department, and Jubilee International Ministries. Tamara Hawthorne has been an active member of Jubilee International Ministries for fourteen years. In 2013, Tamara Hawthorne obtained her Associates Degree in Theology.

Tamara Hawthorne is the wife of her supportive husband, Nathaniel Hawthorne. Mrs. Hawthorne is also the proud mother of one adult daughter and grandmother of her beloved four-year-old grandson.

CITED SOURCES

Webster's New World Dictionary of the American Language, 1982

Strong's Exhaustive Concordance of the Bible, James Strong, Revised, Crusade, 1984

CPSIA information can be obtained at www.ICGtesting.com
Printed in the USA
BVOW05s0941300716

457353BV00001B/1/P